Emerson Lake & Palmer

Pictures at an exhibition

Laura Shenton

Emerson Lake & Palmer

Pictures at an Exhibition

Laura Shenton

WYMER
PUBLISHING
Bedford, England

First published in 2021 by Wymer Publishing
Bedford, England www.wymerpublishing.co.uk Tel: 01234 326691
Wymer Publishing is a trading name of Wymer (UK) Ltd

Copyright © 2021 Laura Shenton / Wymer Publishing.

ISBN: 978-1-912782-67-3 (also available as Kindle eBook).

Edited by Jerry Bloom.

The Author hereby asserts his rights to be identified
as the author of this work in accordance with sections
77 to 78 of the Copyright, Designs & Patents Act 1988.

All rights reserved. No part of this publication may be
reproduced or transmitted in any form or by any means,
electronic or mechanical, including photocopying, or any
information storage and retrieval system, without written
permission from the publisher.

This publication is sold subject to the condition that it shall not,
by way of trade or otherwise, be lent, re-sold, hired out or
otherwise circulated without the publishers' prior consent in any
form of binding or cover other than that in which it is published
and without a similar condition including this condition
being imposed on the subsequent purchaser.

Printed and bound in Great Britain by
CMP, Dorset.

A catalogue record for this book is available from the British Library.

Typeset by Andy Bishop / 1016 Sarpsborg.
Cover design by 1016 Sarpsborg.
Cover photo © Pictorial Press / Alamy Stock Photo.

Contents

Preface	7
Chapter One — *Why Pictures At An Exhibition?*	9
Chapter Two — *The Making Of Pictures At An Exhibition*	36
Chapter Three — *How Does ELP's Version Compare To Mussorgsky's?*	55
Chapter Three — *A Continuing Legacy*	71
A Comprehensive Discography	104
Tour Dates	108

Preface

In many ways, *Pictures At An Exhibition* is the underdog of Emerson, Lake and Palmer's longstanding discography; so much so that there was uncertainty about whether or not it was even going to be released. And yet, despite ELP's uncertainties surrounding the LP at the time that it came to be, the album has become iconic — both in terms of ELP's history and in the wider sense of how it bridged a gap between rock and classical music. It certainly wasn't the first album to do this but it is nevertheless a relevant and important part of such discourse. In terms of the latter and with regards to what ELP did with Mussorgsky's original piece in 1971, *Pictures At An Exhibition* is certainly worthy of its own book. So here it is getting one.

My aim in writing this book is to offer an insight into ELP's *Pictures At An Exhibition* in a way that discusses the music in detail in relation to what the band's intentions were. I want to offer something factual rather than something that is peppered with my own opinion and interpretation of the music. You won't see any of that whole kind of "this section is in the key of C and it therefore means X" or "I think this lyric means Y". As author of this book, it is not my place to throw a lot of my own opinions out there because it won't add anything to the literature if I do that.

The purpose of this book is to look at ELP's *Pictures At An Exhibition* in detail; an extent of detail that has been put out there by ELP in terms of what was intended by the album and detail as in how the album was perceived at the time. As a result, throughout this book you're going to see lots of quotes from vintage articles. I think it's important to corroborate such material as there will probably come a time when it is harder to source.

In the interest of transparency, I have no affiliation with ELP or with any of their associates. This book is based on extensive research and objective commentary. It is a gossip free zone and not about the personal lives of the musicians. That wouldn't be fair, particularly with Keith Emerson and Greg Lake having passed on. This book is about the music.

Chapter One

Why Pictures At An Exhibition?

When Emerson, Lake and Palmer played *Pictures At An Exhibition* live, it was seen as a fun piece of classical music that had mileage in live performances — it was never actually intended to be an album. Consequently, it went on quite a bumpy road in the journey to being released. The irony is that live, it was a substantial part of ELP's sets. In the early days of the band's tenure it was often played in full and towards the later period, part of it served as an encore.

Ultimately, there is a strong contrast between what *Pictures At An Exhibition* means in the context of ELP's legacy and the way it was met with doubt, at times even by the band themselves. In such regard, it is fascinating to consider in-depth what the album means in terms of how it came to be and the barriers that had to be overcome to make such a thing possible.

In order to do this, it is necessary to examine where ELP were at with things from the beginning of their tenure as a newly established band. For they hadn't been going for very long at all when their adaptation of Mussorgsky's iconic piece of classical music was added to their live repertoire.

Lake was quoted in *Beat Instrumental* in January 1971; "If you could imagine the problems that faced this band when we started. We had to live down The Nice for a start, which wasn't easy since we had the main element of The Nice with us. Then, we only had a few weeks to get an act on the road and an album made. It had to be unpretentious and it had to set a direction for all of us at the same time. Incredibly difficult, as you can imagine. We purposely had to avoid doing press, but we knew that eyes were

ELP - *Pictures At An Exhibition*: In-depth

on us and we had to avoid giving people an excuse to accuse us of hype... They seemed to think we'd had it easy. I'd like to meet anyone who thinks *I've* had it easy, for a start. I've worked like bloody hell in this business for years, man, and I've starved. I've slept in vans and all the rest of it. At the moment, I couldn't go out and buy a bloody Ford! That's how rich *I* am!"

In *Melody Maker* in May 1970, Chris Welch reported on what was very early days for ELP; "Being witness to the birth of a band is always an exciting experience, and especially pleasing when the talents consist of three superb musicians like Keith Emerson, Greg Lake, and Carl Palmer. It was a privilege to hear the first tentative steps together of those who quit the security of three established bands — The Nice, King Crimson and Atomic Rooster — at a special preview at a London recording studio. The band had only played four times when I heard them at Island's half-built main studio in an old church in Notting Hill. Their representatives took pains to point out that they had only just started and were not entirely together. But the sounds that emerged were immediately startling and auger well for the future. Surprisingly, when one considers that they are already tipped as a major new force and have been under pressure to appear at this year's galaxy of festivals, the group have been having serious problems, the main one being a place to rehearse. There were several complaints about the noise as they thundered away — Carl 'The Basher' Palmer contributing one of his phenomenal drum solos, Greg buzzing his bass until the floor began to vibrate, and Keith tipping his organ around to obtain the frightening effects he made famous with The Nice. On bearding them in their lair, they were grappling with a piece of contemporary music by Béla Bartók, which sounded quite remarkable in their dextrous hands. They paused for deep conversation about the placing of accents, Keith peering across his grand piano to Carl concentrating furiously on drum patterns... They treated me to a fast and furious version of 'Rondo' with Carl disappearing in a blur of hair and drumsticks as he attacked his snare, bass and tom toms with brutal strength. 'And there's more where that came from', he gasped later. A version of '21st Century

Why *Pictures At An Exhibition*?

Schizoid Man' set my teeth on edge, aggravated by the vibration of the flooring, which in turn caused a stream of complaints from the studio below. They have to work a lot on material and arrangements. But the raw resources are there and when they are ready to explode upon us — BAZONKA! Hey, that's not a bad name for a group." (Emerson played a version of *Pictures At An Exhibition* on the organ at Chris Welch's wedding on 4th December 1971. It was included among a choice of traditional hymns).

Greg Lake reminisced in his (posthumously published) autobiography in 2017; "From the very first few bars we played together, I could sense there was a very special chemistry between the three of us. We started with 'Rondo', which Keith had adapted from Dave Brubeck's jazz classic, 'Blue Rondo à la Turk', for The Nice's first album."

Following several rehearsal sessions at Island Studios in Notting Hill, ELP established their initial live set. It consisted of 'The Barbarian', 'Rondo', 'Nut Rocker' and *Pictures At An Exhibition*. Notably, *Pictures* wasn't the only piece that was strongly inspired by classical music. 'The Barbarian' is an arrangement of a piano suite by Béla Bartók and 'Rondo' is an arrangement of Dave Brubeck's jazz standard, 'Blue Rondo à la Turk' (Emerson had already recorded a version of it with The Nice). ELP's intention to use classical music as a strong point of reference in their music was prominent from the very beginning. Emerson was quoted in *Beetle* in February 1974; "I realised I liked the classics after really liking jazz. I realised there was a similarity between the two — all jazz pianists were listening to the classics. People like Bill Evans and Dave Brubeck were obviously listening to the classics, with their counterpoint themes, and adaptations of Bach. So I started going back to my old Bach books after that, and working them out myself."

Emerson was certain that he wanted to play a version of *Pictures At An Exhibition* after hearing Mussorgsky's piece performed with an orchestra. In the 2016 released deluxe edition of ELP's *Pictures At An Exhibition*, Chris Welch quoted Emerson on how he first encountered Mussorgsky's piece. Emerson and his wife attended a concert at London's South Bank. Of which Emerson was quoted; "We happened to be walking past the Royal Festival Hall and I got us some tickets for that day's concert. We had balcony seats overlooking the audience and the orchestra. The first piece was *The Wasps* by Vaughan Williams and the second was *Pictures At An Exhibition*." Following this, Emerson then went to Chappell & Co. music publishers in Bond Street to access a score of the latter. He was quoted in the same liner notes; "The guy behind the counter knew me and said, 'Why do you want the orchestration?' I explained I wanted to transcribe it to piano. He gave me a stunned look at said 'Do you not realise sir this was originally a piano solo piece that Ravel orchestrated?' Poor old Mussorgsky never got to know about the orchestration of his work."

Upon purchasing a copy of the score and improvising around the piece in the studio, Lake and Palmer agreed that is was a good idea to do an adaptation of *Pictures* as part of their live set, but only their live set. With regards to how ELP's version of *Pictures At An Exhibition* came about, Greg Lake explained in his autobiography; "In the very early days of ELP, Keith suggested that we could do our own version live and both Carl and I really liked the idea. It quickly became one of the signatures of our live performances but we had never recorded it in the studio."

Carl Palmer was quoted in *Record Collector* in February 2014; "I'd been listening to that piece of music since I was seven years old, and to produce it in a live environment was the best way to do it. The excitement is there, which might have been impossible to capture in a studio. Keith loved the music too, so we started playing it at rehearsals. Day by day it got bigger, it went on and on, and we finally had it. It was a natural progression."

He was quoted in *Prog* in May 2017; "Keith and I had this thing, that we really enjoyed classical music. I come from a really classical background, with my father being a professor of music and so on, and so Keith and I always used to rib each other, 'Have you heard this?' and 'Have you heard that?' We'd be talking about

Why Pictures At An Exhibition?

various pieces of music and something would come up, and I'd say, 'I used to listen to that at home with my grandfather!' So there was a bit of synergy going on there straight away."

In the 2016 liner notes of ELP's *Pictures At An Exhibition*, Chris Welch quoted Lake; "I remember the first time we played it. We were in the rehearsal room and had been talking about the idea. Then Keith came to rehearsals and he'd just got the score. Before we started playing he'd warm up on the piano by playing *Pictures*. I sat there with my bass and played along. ELP was all about rehearsal. We used to refine these ideas and that's what made it come together with accuracy. Keith and I played the piece together and after a while Carl joined in and it sounded quite good. So we realised it could be made into something. Then one day we decided to do it in concert, like a dare. Keith said to me 'let's play it live'. So we did and it went down a storm. It was meant to happen."

The band's first live gig took place on 23rd August 1970 at the Plymouth Guildhall. A local band by the name of Earth was the support act. It was reported in *New Musical Express* in August 1970; "Emerson, Lake and Palmer made their world debut on Sunday at Plymouth Guildhall. The group strolled on stage looking somewhat nervous, somewhat apprehensive. They'd been rehearsing for four months and this was the test. 'This is what we sound like', said Keith Emerson, and the group launched into 'Barbarian', a thundering wall of sound with Keith playing two Hammond organs at the same time and Greg Lake pumping at his fuzz bass. The music had a feeling of power, of indestructible strength and the capacity audience were unleashed. Then 'Take A Pebble', a more fragile number with Keith plucking at the piano strings and then Greg switching to acoustic guitar, his voice floating out smoothly with Keith now on electric harpsichord. Next, a forty-minute composition, aptly titled *Pictures At An Exhibition*, a series of musical paintings and musical modes. *Pictures* saw the debut of the Moog synthesiser, weird electric sounds, sometimes harsh and angry and sometimes soft and soothing. Throughout, Carl Palmer bent over his drums, sometimes smiling at Greg who stood solid like a three-hundred-year oak tree. Emerson's showmanship was exceptional as he attacked his instruments in an orgy of visual excitement. Suddenly *Pictures* was over and the group were walking off stage, sweating and happy. The audience wanted more, much more. E. L. and P. returned and 'Rondo' — tighter and more forceful than ever before — blasted out. Then another encore. 'Remember this?' said Keith, as he led into 'Nut Rocker' once more. As Keith, Greg and Carl finally walked off, shirtless and exhausted, the audience stood on their chairs shouting, clapping, whistling, stamping their feet. For a full quarter of an hour the hopeful shouts of 'more, more' filled the concert hall. Emerson, Lake and Palmer had arrived."

Palmer was quoted in *Kent News* in May 2012; "Our first show was at the Plymouth Guildhall, ahead of the Isle of Wight Festival of August 1970. It only held about 430 people, so it was a pretty small venue. But we went down a storm and earned around £400."

It was still relatively humble beginnings though; ELP travelled to the gig in a transit van that had previously been owned by Yes. The logic behind playing in a small venue outside of London was to ensure that if things didn't go well on the night, embarrassment would be less public and ideally, minimised. Fortunately though, the gig went well.

Greg Lake explained in his autobiography; "Having a good deal of experience in playing live shows with our previous bands, we had the good sense to insist on having our inaugural show somewhere a bit more out of the way and less conspicuous, so the very first show of ELP took place in front of eight hundred people at the Guildhall in Plymouth on Sunday 23rd August 1970. We were nervous. I had barely performed in front of an audience since December 1969 and Carl and Keith had both been away from the stage for a few months too. And here we were, playing live together for the very first time as well as playing material no one had ever heard before — 'The Barbarian', 'Take A Pebble' and the full length three quarters of an hour version of *Pictures At An Exhibition* as well as 'Rondo'. Keith kicked off the concert

Why Pictures At An Exhibition?

with the simple words, 'This is what we sound like'. We ended up getting a fifteen-minute standing ovation and I felt a deep sense of relief as I drove back home to London."

ELP's second gig was on the 29th August in 1970 at the Isle of Wight Festival. Emerson had put in a memorable performance there with The Nice the previous year and in some ways, the pressure was on. In the *Middlesex County Press* in September 1970, it was reported that "Nearly half a million people from Britain, Europe and America braved the cold nights and lived in near-primitive conditions to listen to some of today's top musicians at the Isle of Wight Festival. A town of its own had been created where total freedom reigned. Pseudo-hippies who were frowned upon in suburbia found thousands and thousands like themselves. Now, the group of holidaymakers taking strolls though 'Freedom City' between their hotel meals felt out of place. Many people came unprepared for sleeping in the open. The St. John Ambulance dealt with hundreds of people suffering from exposure, and hot soup was dished out to shivering thousands. Sanitation was appalling. The only available lavatories consisted of trenches surrounded by corrugated fences. If you were one of the thousands who paid to go into the main arena and ended up a quarter-mile from the stage, then you probably wasted your money. The best view was free — from East Aston Down, nicknamed 'Devastation Hill'. Many French and Germans who believed that pop festivals should be free camped here. Ironically they proved to be right, as a cool easterly wind was blowing throughout, taking sounds up the hill. Many people who had bought three-day tickets for £3 discovered this and tried to sell them at the entrance gate. The organisers, Fiery Creations, retaliated by telling people not to buy tickets at the main gain because a number had been forged. The island burst into sound on the Wednesday and thousands who had been camping outside moved into the arena for a free show lasting until early Friday morning. Except for Black Widow, all were little-known groups. Friday was the first fee-paying day with Chicago, Family, Taste and Procol Harum taking the limelight. On Saturday, Tiny Tim wooed the audience with his falsetto rendition

ELP - *Pictures At An Exhibition*: In-depth

of 'Tiptoe Through The Tulips' and 'There'll Always Be An England'."

The feature continued; "Performances from Emerson, Lake and Palmer went down well, as did John Sebastian, Ten Years After, The Doors, Sly and the Family Stone and, of course, The Who, whose wild rhythmic sound does not seem to have changed much since their unknown days, playing in Harrow about seven years ago. By Sunday the festival grounds had become squalid. Waste abounded and water from the loos mixed with the mud to form a marshy expanse. The Jimi Hendrix Experience managed to get thousands out of their sleeping bags to dance in the night. It was an incredible sight. People, waving their arms in the air, were silhouetted against the smoke-filled sky. Then the soft, plaintive sounds of Joan Baez and Leonard Cohen — the last two acts — sent the ravers to sleep again. People listened to the music huddled together in sleeping bags. Others had rugs to keep them warm. Despite bad stage management, with gaps of sometimes half an hour between acts, the fans were appreciative. The artists were flops if their finale came without the shout of 'more, more!'. The beach at Freshwater Bay provided an occasional haven from the music. Here hundreds of boys and girls stripped off to sun and sea bathe. Drug pushers in the crowd came straight out with 'want any acid, man?' while plain clothes detectives dressed like hippies pounded their beat through Freedom City. This tactic proved unpopular but effective. A collection for those who had been 'busted' raised £16,000. Many stallholders ruthlessly exploited the crowd as demand exceeded supply. Peaches were a shilling each. Eleven penny yoghurts went for 1s 6d and shilling cans of coke were sold for double the price. Despite objections the festival was a success, and as one of the residents said: 'It's marvellous to see so many people enjoying themselves. It's proved the old colonels wrong who said the island would be wrecked'."

Whilst the report didn't put the spotlight on ELP, it really sets the scene in terms of what the Isle of Wight Festival perhaps felt like in 1970. The sensory elements of the festival are really brought to life by the way the journalist described the event and it

Why Pictures At An Exhibition?

certainly shows the scale of the crowd that ELP performed to at a key appearance in their career. Lake was quoted in *Classic Rock* in October 2007; "The enduring memory is the actual physical sight of that many people. I suppose before that, the only time you'd see that many people gathered together would have been a war. The night before, we'd played to something like 1000 people. The next day it was 600,000... There was a kind of random chaos taking place. In a way, it was all meant to be relaxed and 'peace, love, and have a nice day' but there was a kind of tension about the whole thing."

The scale of the festival was such that it drew a lot of attention to ELP. Lake was quoted of the Isle of Wight Festival in *Classic Rock* in October 2007; "After that festival, the very next day ELP was on the front page of every music newspaper. It was indeed one of those overnight sensations." It was reported in *New Musical Express* in August 1970 under the headline of "Isle Of Wight Stars"; "Two of the saddest events in pop music during the past few months have been the breakup of The Nice and various members of King Crimson leaving to go their own ways. But out of that has come something brand new and very promising — Emerson, Lake and Palmer."

Greg Lake recalled of the Isle of Wight Festival in his autobiography; "We were extremely excited to have this incredible opportunity so early on in the band's career, but at the same time we were quite nervous about playing at such a big event before we even had a chance to get the show broken in and under control. In this sense, it really was a trial by fire."

Skilled showmen that they were and not ones to miss an opportunity, Emerson and Lake set off cannons at the end of *Pictures At An Exhibition*. Prior to the performance, Emerson had tested the cannons in a field that was close to Heathrow Airport. Lake enthused in his autobiography on how at "the very end of our experimental arrangement of *Pictures At An Exhibition*, when Keith and I triggered the two cannons on stage, it was an unbelievable once in a lifetime moment when the entire audience rose to their feet and gave the band a standing ovation."

ELP - *Pictures At An Exhibition*: In-depth

Lake was quoted in *Classic Rock* in October 2007; "We decided to fire these nineteenth century cannons at the end of *Pictures At An Exhibition* — to emulate the *1812 Overture*. Unknown to us, the road crew had doubled the charge in the cannons. All I can remember was seeing this huge, solid-iron cannon leave the ground! It blew a couple of people off the stage. Luckily there was no cannonball in it. Thank God!"

Eccentric showmanship indeed! Familiar territory for Emerson though. A former manager of Emerson's when he was with The Nice, Tony Stratton-Smith, was quoted in *The New York Times* in December 1973; "When they started, Keith was apt to hide at the back of the stage behind the organ, tuck himself into the shadows. But when The Nice started as a solo act, Keith decided that somebody had to do something, had to be a showman. They thought that people wouldn't just listen to the music. So Keith started all the leaping about, standing on his Hammond organ, cracking whips and sticking knives into the instrument. I don't believe he was into actually throwing knives at that time. I don't think he thought his aim was all that and he needed more practice. That came later."

Emerson's gimmick of sticking knives into the Hammond wasn't just for dramatic effect though; it had a purpose in how it allowed him to hold down a chord, freeing his fingers to move to other parts of the keyboard.

All in a day's work! Emerson was quoted in *Crawdaddy* in August 1971; "I got an electric shock out the back of the organ once and it gave me a big scar and I also stabbed my thumb in Boston. It looked quite good, blood all over the keys and I didn't mop it up for about a month, the contrast of the red blood against the white keyboard." Lake was quoted in the same feature; "Well, at the end of a performance they (the audience) should be exhausted and they should be really happy with what they've seen, that's what we aim for."

Emerson was quoted on the theatrical elements of being on stage in *Circus* in March 1972; "I've gone on and I've played and I've not done any theatrics at all and it's gone down just as well,

Why Pictures At An Exhibition?

so I have a choice really of doing it or not doing it. It all started (the whole thing wasn't planned) out of being exhilarated onstage and reaching a point where the music was no longer sufficient to reach a climax. There weren't notes good enough to go above what you wanted to do and that's the point where I started going into this other medium, the visual side. The way I look on the stage act now is creation and destruction. The visual side of the act does become destructive art. The fact that we're creating right from the start can only reach a certain peak musically. That's why I'm sort of into destructive art; that's what Pete Townsend is into anyway. It's a whole sort of thing with The Who. I think there's a place for destructive art in music. Music is generally a release and whatever way a musician chooses to do it, whether visually or musically, I don't think it matters as long as the music comes out the same and everything I do which can be considered as a theatrical does a certain function in the music. The fact that I choose to ride an organ across the stage has a function in the music. I could get the same effect if I stood there and shook the instrument, because what is happening is the reverberation unit in the back is crashing and making a big explosive sound. I could do the same thing by standing in one place and rocking the organ, but I get the same effect out of riding it across the stage, so why not do it? Using knives in the act came from when The Nice were doing 'America' and in 'America' (on *Ars Longa Vita Brevis*) I wanted to hold down two notes and sustain a fifth while I was playing another organ. I started out by using pegs, just wooden things to hold down the keys. Then I thought I could do the same thing with knives and if I'm playing 'America,' the music from *West Side Story*, then the knives have a definite part in it, being connected with the film and the gang fights. So I thought, 'yes, it has a place here,' and then I used to take the knives out of the keyboard and throw them on the floor; and then probably one night I decided to throw them at the cabinets. It has a place in the music. I mean if I rode an organ across the stage and there wasn't anything coming out of it, that would be ridiculous."

The predominant narrative of ELP's history today seems to

ELP - *Pictures At An Exhibition*: In-depth

be that the Isle of Wight Festival was a dead cert in putting the band on the road to success but actually, at the time they received mixed reviews. As a result, there were a number of interviews in which the group were keen to assert what their creative intentions were and what the impact of the negative press had, had on them.

It was asserted in *Beat Instrumental* in January 1971; "To weld together a group of this stature, accomplishment and potential is extremely difficult. Greg Lake, although naturally hurt by some of the more waspish critics is more sad than angry at their failure to perceive something fresh and new." To which Lake was quoted; "The pity is that now is the most beautiful time to catch anything, in its early days. The energy is vital and alive, and this is when people ought to be enthusiastic. It's like a flower just coming up through the earth. You go SMASH! Like that, it'll still live, it'll crawl around under the surface for a while, because it's got strength in the roots, and it'll come up again. But you've missed the beauty of the first push through."

It was reported in the same feature; "Almost immediately afterwards (post Plymouth Guildhall gig), it was Isle of Wight time and, like many another artist, they received mixed receptions. Some raved, others scoffed. The more notorious pundits of the musical press inflated their outraged egos and let fly. Others, less rigid in their outlook, saw beyond the apathetic vibes of the 'Festival' — but there is no doubt that ELP were wounded by the mainly negative press of their first international appearance."

Lake was quoted of the Isle of Wight gig in *Melody Maker* in February 1971; "We put on a bad performance and we were setting ourselves up for judgement. That would have been okay if we had played well but we couldn't because the festival itself was so badly organised — the PA and everything — and we rely so much on the equipment being just right. The criticism there was just, but it was still poor. If they had written in the papers that the band played a bad set because the conditions were not right — but they didn't. After that we sort of got scrubbed out and nobody took any notice. The good part about the band was just left unnoticed and it is a source of pride to us that the LP sold

Why Pictures At An Exhibition?

an incredible amount of records, and we didn't push it or hype it in there. It was just bought by people who dug us on the tour... I had expected criticism, but it is still a hard pill to swallow. It gets through to you. But I think we have now gone through the stage where people are judging us. And really, I don't hold it against anybody who scratched us."

This extent of pressure on ELP and anxiety about the press was an ongoing theme at times. Lake was quoted in *Disc & Music Echo* in July 1971; "We must be the hardest working band. I've never had this amount of pressure before. It's good because we're successful. But it's bad because our nerves suffer. One minute you open a paper and see your album's number one, the next your hands are shaking. It's that sort of pressure."

So really, with hindsight, it would seem that the Isle of Wight Festival had been an excellent vehicle for ELP to expand their publicity but it also perhaps left them with a sense of needing to defy some of the weird and wonderful things said by the press at the time. Not only were there negative reviews that may have inspired a need to prove the critics wrong but also, on the flip side, a label of supergroup was being bandied about and this too put pressure on the band.

Greg Lake asserted in his autobiography; "We never had the chance to develop the band organically before we were being labelled. ELP were often portrayed as if we had all been born with silver spoons in our mouths, which of course was a very long way from the truth. All three members of ELP had spent many hard years in former bands sleeping in the back of vans and quite literally living on the breadline. We had paid our dues in the early days in order to get to where we were, so this tag of being a supergroup was not something we either wanted or felt good about. It was this tag, added to the fact that a lot of the music we played had European classical roots, that probably gave some people the impression that we were being pretentious or high-minded. It was certainly true that we were ambitious and we did want to be original and innovative. However, at no time did we ever claim to be classical musicians or even classically trained musicians. We were just British rock and roll musicians drawing a large part of our influence from European rather than American roots. For us, it seemed important at the time to try and break away from the same old tried and tested path that so many other British rock acts had followed in the past by using American blues, rock and roll and gospel music as their sole source of inspiration."

There is certainly a difference between a person wanting to be seen as a super something — group or star! — and wanting to be recognised for their efforts. Lake was quoted in *Melody Maker* in February 1971; "Tell me, why is it that bass players go largely unnoticed? I feel sorry for all bass players — there are some good ones around. The trouble is I never got credit for what I did in King Crimson. Most of the songs on that album (the first) I had a large part in creating. 'Schizoid Man' — I wrote the riff and the song, 'Epitaph'. I wrote the melody line for 'In The Court Of The Crimson King'. The things I do are like parts that make up something but don't necessarily form a large part of the end product. It comes back to the unnoticed bass player. Take him away and see how he's noticed. I feel frustrated that my output has to do with the total thing rather than one specific part. I am not really after that superstar recognition. I don't want to be a solo superstar. I know that sounds corny but the motive I have for being successful is that I want to move people emotionally and I would dig to have enough money to be secure. Yet it is annoying when you don't get credit for what you do."

Whilst still finding their groove with the public and the media, ELP needed to play their cards right with it still being early days. Lake was quoted in *Melody Maker* in February 1971; "You have to be super aware all the time. Nothing you do can be at all flash because any hole you leave anywhere, people will be jumping in to tear the heart out of you. When I think of all the good ideas that got thrown out — we were so afraid of being thought flash about it all."

It was considered in *Rock & Pop Superstar* in May 1979; "The first live show of the band was on August 23rd, 1970, in Plymouth Guild Hall even though, actually, it had been a preparation to the

Why Pictures At An Exhibition?

official beginning of the group at the Isle of Wight Festival. Since its beginning its music was an incredible gig, celebrating their first show in the Festival with cannons and Emerson presenting his new Moog synthesiser unfolding to the plot an entire series of acrobatics, stabbing the organs and other violent demonstrations. Not all critics liked this kind of music. Famous English DJ John Peel said: 'A waste of talent and electricity'. In every way, the public recognised the new giant divided in three (and multiplied by three) and that indicated that the market was prepared for the release of their first LP. Called simply, *Emerson, Lake and Palmer* and presenting a dove with the wings opened was a clear demonstration of the potential of the group with 'The Barbarian' hardness, the delicate chords of Lake in 'Take A Pebble' and 'Lucky Man' and Emerson's and Palmer's wonderful performance in 'The Three Fates' and 'Tank' respectively. The album placed the band among the biggest hopes of English music of the new decade."

It was certainly the case that ELP were invested in making the band a long term success. Lake was quoted in *Disc & Music Echo* in July 1971; "When we formed the band we had a very definite idea of what we wanted it to be. And we knew that we wanted it to last for a long time. We could have had a short, quick smash and cleaned-up moneywise. But we still dig to play. If I was writing on my own I could probably get into many and varied things. But I don't feel restricted within this band. I write with and for the band. When you write music, as with any other art, it depends a lot on your environment. As ELP is my environment my writing is geared to it. If I was in a folk-duo I would write differently. No, it's not restricting, but, to a certain extent, I'm governed. Carl plays a bigger part in arranging. Often something in 3/4 will end up in 5/4 when The Palmer gets at it. It's hard to say who does what because we all tend to muscle in with ideas."

Upon being asked whether ELP's first album was a statement of intent, Carl Palmer was quoted *Record Collector* in February 2014; "I don't think the first album really said that's how we are. Keith Emerson wanted to play three organ pieces, which had no relation to the group at all, really. It didn't involve the other members, and I thought that was rather strange. There was a song thrown in at the end called 'Lucky Man', because we were short on time, and that turned out to be a big hit. Keith and I wrote 'Tank', which was a nice coming together. It was a bit of a hodgepodge, but because it was so quintessentially English, and because it was so different, it did catch on. There was one very strong rock track, 'Knife-Edge'. It all came together very quickly. I think that it was recorded in two weeks."

Greg Lake explained in his autobiography; "When ELP was formed, such was the buzz around the band that expectations were very quickly flying high and within days we were being asked for a date when we thought we could deliver the first album."

ELP's first album and indeed the single from it, 'Lucky Man' were, in some ways, unlikely successes. 'Lucky Man' is just over four and a half minutes long — this would have made it something of a risk in terms of getting radio play. Also, the track showcases an unusual range of instrumentation in that it contains a Moog solo. Not only that, but a Moog solo that makes liberal use of portamento (pitch sliding from one note to another).

Essentially, 'Lucky Man' is a very unique sounding track and it is plausible that the odds may have been against it commercially but nevertheless the single helped to sell the album. The Moog was a distinctive feature throughout. Greg Lake confirmed of the track, 'Take A Pebble', when responding to a readers question in *Melody Maker* in October 1971; "The pebble sound was achieved on the Moog synthesiser. We used reverb on it to get a sound like water dripping in a cave."

Emerson was quoted of the *Emerson, Lake and Palmer* album in *Beetle* in February 1974; "Atlantic records decided to release it ('Lucky Man') in America. We were in England at the time before we knew about it. I wasn't too pleased about it, but the way it goes the records are usually handed out to the DJs and they play the ones they like and they use the shortest ones. It's quite a commercial song to an extent and it's possibly from that point of view that it was used. It's quite easy to relate to. It was never

Why Pictures At An Exhibition?

released in England. I didn't have any pre-conceived ideas about it (the first ELP album) doing that well. Something like 'Knife-Edge' would have been a bit more representative at the time. That was right at the beginning, we had no choice. I hadn't even met the people from Atlantic, because we were still in England. It was only after I got to America that I realised that it had been out and that it had done this and it had done that. Atlantic were pleased because it was selling the album. A lot of people liked it, they were obviously buying it. It was really the people's choice. It is a shame that we really can't perform it the same way it is on the album. There's a lot of double tracked vocals. Greg's playing electric, bass and acoustic guitar on it. If we had really thought about it, and we ourselves, had wanted to release it as a single, then we would have considered these points, and possibly re-arranged it so we could have done it some way on stage. Now we come out and people want to hear it. Greg performs it as an acoustic piece and I guess its rather disappointing to some people because they want to hear the recorded version. There we were, in the position of it having been released and us not knowing that people want to hear it, and the way it was done on the album being impossible for us to do on stage. It's a throw-in thing."

In the US, ELP's debut eponymous album was released in the spring of 1971 by Atlantic's Cotillion label. It was met with much critical acclaim and was in the top twenty on the album chart by March.

On the first ELP album, it is evident that Emerson was influenced by Béla Bartók. Emerson said as much himself in a number of interviews and the percussive use of piano on ELP's first album very much showcases this. Their eponymous debut album was reviewed in the *Reading Evening Post* in December 1970; "The last twelve months have seen fantastic exchanges in the world of so-called popular musicianship and composition has improved almost out of recognition, and the divisions of classic, jazz and pop under which the less enlightened record departments love to list their wares has narrowed to be almost ridiculous. Never were these facts better illustrated than on this absolutely superb album. Although the three titles on side one are sufficient evidence of the trio's outstanding talent, it is 'The Three Fates' suite on the reverse that really takes one's breath away. After only a single hearing I'd rank it among my top three records of the year."

It was advocated in the *Coventry Evening Telegraph* in December 1970; "Emerson, Lake and Palmer are choice among the progressive groups on the college circuit. Their self-titled LP on Island shows why. The music is sufficiently unusual to be distinctive yet it has enough to be consistently appealing."

It was considered in the *Newcastle Journal* in December 1970; "Keith Emerson, organist with The Nice, is moving on to still greater things with the help of guitarist Greg Lake (ex-King Crimson) and Carl Palmer (ex-Atomic Rooster). The trio's first Island album is already high in the charts, as it richly deserves to be. The three-part suite that opens the second side of the LP is an imaginative exercise in fusing classical music and jazz-pop, with Emerson on top form on the Royal Festival Hall organ. When he masters his Moog synthesiser, there should be no stopping them."

It was considered in *Beat Instrumental* in January 1971; "Emerson's classical influences are still there, of course. It takes more than a few months to subdue such a dominant musical trait. Nevertheless, it is easy to hear that the more melodic character of Lake's music is already making itself felt. On the *Emerson, Lake and Palmer* album (which has confounded the earlier pundits by proving and infuriatingly massive seller) there is a composition called 'Take A Pebble', in which Greg shows himself the originator of the softer side of ELP. Written and sung by Lake, 'Take A Pebble' opens with brushed chords on piano strings, leading into gentle bass and lyrics from Greg. These, in turn, evolve into an expounded development on piano from Keith, finally returning to a re-statement of the opening theme. Keith's piano playing is just one of the many surprises on this album. It seems to be his natural instrument — even more than the organ — and he makes use of some highly original and creative work, sounding almost Gershwin-esque at times in his efforts to combine classism,

Why Pictures At An Exhibition?

romanticism and twentieth century modes. On organ, however, Emerson returns to his best-known forte, and 'Knife-Edge', the heaviest number on the LP, gives him chance to catch the pulse of the listener with his unique and demoniac style. 'Knife-Edge' is, in some ways, the most representative ELP sound (as it appears in this album). Brooding, fierce and frightening, it is a vocal showcase for Lake, as well as a complete vehicle for the more percussive talents of both Carl Palmer and Keith Emerson."

ELP's debut album was reviewed in the *Buckinghamshire Examiner* in December 1970; "Emerson, Lake and Palmer are names that have been bandied around pop critic circles for a long time. Everyone has been expecting so much from their debut album. And now it is on sale there is a wave of criticism directed at the band. This is probably a good thing because the band are so good and total acceptance from the start might well stunt their growth. Now they can study themselves in the harsh and painful glare of adverse opinion. Carl's drumming is so different from his work with Atomic Rooster. His power and technique have been channelled, and he is so much looser and more inventive. Keith Emerson seems to be getting more into contemporary classics and is vaguely similar to Stan Kenton. He is one of a few who come anywhere near exploring the full possibilities of the Moog. The first side has three songs — 'The Barbarian', 'Take A Pebble' and 'Knife-Edge'. Here we have the chance of hearing Greg's folksy voice and acoustic guitar. Side two opens with church organ on 'The Three Fates', Keith doing his *Phantom Of The Opera* bit, dissolving into more beautiful piano. Emerson, Lake and Palmer have so much to say and offer. It would be a tragedy if they were stifled or discouraged by the knockers. They could become moodies."

The review really highlights the fact that upon the release of their debut album, ELP were in a very tentative position; whilst the album largely received positive critical acclaim and commercial success, it was still very early days. In such regard, it is understandable as to why there was a sense of uncertainly about whether or not *Pictures At An Exhibition* should be released as an album. It is plausible that there was an element of risk due to it being a live performance of something that Emerson himself considered was done predominantly for fun.

Emerson, Lake and Palmer all had a wealth of commercial achievements behind them already as individuals by the time they formed a band together. This may have perhaps helped to promote their debut album as a new group.

"Emerson, Lake and Palmer, who have signed with Island Records and have their first LP out in November (featuring such items as 'The Barbarian' and 'Take A Pebble') are, of course, Keith Emerson, Greg Lake and Carl Palmer who appear at the City Hall on Sunday (October 4th)," reported the *Newcastle Evening Chronicle* in October 1970. "No self-respecting pop fan should need to be reminded that Keith (ex Gary Farr and the T Bones, and VIP's) really made a name for himself with The Nice, or that he was voted top international keyboard player in *Melody Maker*'s widely respected poll. Greg Lake was with King Crimson, who became the talking point of the Rolling Stones' free Hyde Park concert last year, and Carl Palmer joined Emerson and Lake via Chris Farlowe and The Thunderbirds, the Crazy World of Arthur Brown and an outfit called Atomic Rooster. The three make a formidable combination and Emerson, Lake and Palmer strike me as being well able to live up to having been voted the most promising new group in the aforementioned poll."

Everyone in ELP brought a high level of skill and professionalism to the table. As individuals they had all been performing from a young age. With Greg Lake being a founding member of King Crimson, Carl Palmer having been with the Crazy World of Arthur Brown and with Keith coming from The Nice, the musicians that went on to form ELP were already established in their field. There was probably also a sense that all three musicians inspired each other to keep getting better and better.

Emerson was quoted in *Crawdaddy* in August 1971; "I had piano lessons at the age of eight until the age of fifteen and that gave me a classical grounding, and at the age of fifteen until about the age of nineteen I had an interest in jazz in which I used to

Why Pictures At An Exhibition?

listen to records and from the age of nineteen, twenty I developed a style which was like a combination of those two things which I'd learned." It was in the same feature that Emerson stated he was around the age of eighteen or nineteen when he started to have an understanding of style, harmony and the general mathematics of music.

Palmer was quoted in *Circus* in September 1972; "I'm pleased I've got speed, but I don't concentrate on it. If I wanted to impress with speed I could play even faster — or make it appear faster. I want to concentrate on my reading and my style." Whilst every member of ELP could read music, they all had their own ways of working with it. Emerson was quoted in *Crawdaddy* in August 1971; "I write out my things, personally. Greg has his own form of shorthand he uses for his bass parts."

Palmer was quoted in *Circus* in March 1972; "I've always worked with organists, you see. Before I met Keith I never thought of working with him. For one thing, I didn't know him. And I was doing my own sort of scene, you know. I'd rather always work with an organ than guitar, because I find guitar sort of limiting to play with unless it's someone like Hendrix, you know. I've always played with a keyboard instrument. I played with Chris Farlowe and the Thunderbirds when I was fifteen. That was soul, yeah, that was a blues band, a soul band with saxophones and everything. It was fun. Even before Farlowe, I was with a band called The Locomotive which had an organ. I started when I was eleven… You sort of get something from everyone you know. The way I play is the way I play, I just sort of got into different things. I've never played with anyone who had classical influences before Keith. Playing with Keith gives me a different aspect; my drumming is slightly sweeter now. My drumming was very brutal with Arthur Brown and with Atomic Rooster. It's a lot subtler now. Playing with a bass player like Greg Lake is a lot different than with Arthur Brown. With Arthur the bass player was very rigid. Playing with someone like Keith is an advantage. I don't lose any of my musical background in this band, you see, which is one of the main factors as a musician to me. All the stages I've gone through, I can apply them all and then more. Vincent Crane (of Atomic Rooster) was very much a blues musician, so I couldn't develop a jazz style or rock drumming style, which is what I'm trying to do now. Keith's organ playing and piano playing have helped me develop the jazz and rock approach, which is what I wanted. Only I didn't know I wanted it until I played with him. Playing with him for that reason is an advantage — and I love him."

Emerson was quoted in *Beetle* in February 1974; "Carl proved that he was more than a rock 'n' roll drummer. He loves jazz. He'd been to music school whereas I hadn't. Everyone seems to think I have. I think it's about time I just said that I did not go to music school. It was some big rumour. The funny thing was that I had all this bullshit written about every organist that came out after that — Oh, he's been to London College of Music, he's got a diploma. It was like an advertisement you had to have. That's ridiculous. Erroll Garner doesn't read music. I read music but only because my music teacher at the time taught me to."

It was asserted in *Beat Instrumental* in January 1971; "Musically, they make valid and equal contributions. It is, of course, difficult for Keith Emerson not to dominate any musical unit of which he is a part. Greg Lake's contributions, although less pyrotechnic, are just as vital. His careful bass patterns, his clear and powerful lyrics and his thoughtful and sensitive handling of the quieter moments are all important and necessary parts of the ELP structure. Carl Palmer's speed and technique are already matters of controversy. Although, like the other two, he sometimes seems to make it seem too easy, in fact he is constantly working — touching a cymbal here, feeling a foot pedal break there. Every nerve in his body seems to be invisibly wired for sound, and his alertness enables him to successfully anticipate the complex patterns of sound that issue from the two musicians on either side of him. In the field of brushwork (which is sadly neglected by too many otherwise competent percussionists), he is a master."

There is a sense that even in the early days of their career, ELP were comfortable with how they preferred to work. Lake was quoted in *Crawdaddy* in August 1971; "We don't rehearse

Why *Pictures At An Exhibition*?

the performance part. We've played in other bands. Performance is a thing you build up over all your career. Every artist does tricks and things, you just build them up. It would look stupid if you just stood rigid and played. Some people take it a little further. Hendrix took it a little further than most people. Keith takes it further than, say, I do. It just depends on how much energy you've got. With me, it's not so much of a physical energy, because I haven't got much of that, it's sort of a mental energy. I get very nervous before going on stage and then when I go out I can feel physically drained, almost exhausted, because I just build up to it. I get too nervous."

To which Emerson was quoted; "The thing with me is my nervous energy gets my adrenalin going which gives me a buzz before I go on, and therefore the bigger and more important the gig the more nervous I get. Those gigs, I get a lot more physically exhausted playing but I usually get a lot more ideas happening in my head. Sometimes I get both going at once; I get a lot of physical energy and a lot of ideas and those gigs get off great. I don't always get the two things happening."

Considering that ELP's *Pictures At An Exhibition* was typically presented as a forty-five minute piece, it was noteworthy to critics that it held an audience's attention. But of course, there is a lot of variety throughout the piece in terms of the instrumentation, moods and styles of each section. It is certainly a worthy piece in its own right and in some ways perhaps, it may have been immune from being disregarded as just another prog rock long song due to the fact that really, it consists of many unique and easily memorable sections.

Released in the UK on Island Records in November 1971, by the following month, *Pictures At An Exhibition* got to number three in the charts. At the time the album was released, budget albums were allowed to be counted as part of the UK album chart but by the beginning of 1972, this was not the case. As a result, *Pictures* was removed from the chart after five weeks where it was then sitting at position number nine. In America, *Pictures At An Exhibition* reached number ten on the Billboard album chart

ELP - *Pictures At An Exhibition*: In-depth

in early 1972.

Not only was *Pictures At An Exhibition* a cheap album to make, but it was also sold at a lower price than studio albums at the time. This was a rational decision. It's hard to imagine today but in general, live albums were often considered as throwaway, inferior products (in fact Deep Purple's live album *Made in Japan*, released in late 1972, wasn't just named so because of where it was recorded but in the early seventies, things made in Japan were considered inferior and it was titled as such in jest).

With studio time being expensive, recording a live album (with minimal studio time required for mixing) presented an opportunity for a higher profit margin in selling the *Pictures* LP at a price that was more in line with other studio albums. And yet, in keeping with the views at the time it was felt that the album needed to be sold for less.

Lester Bangs reviewed *Pictures At An Exhibition* in *Rolling Stone* in March 1972; "If there's one thing you've gotta give ELP, it's balls. Not only did they take one of the most staid standards from the annals of 'serious' music and do it in an amped up electronic version that must drive freaks wild, but they added their own elaborations and improvisations and lyrics as well. Compared to this, the conceit and tastelessness involved in Jon Lord's *Gemini Suite* or the *Concerto For Group And Orchestra* he and Deep Purple performed with the Royal Philharmonic were nothing, the modest work of quiet craftsmen. Emerson, Lake & Palmer are bombastic and tasteless and they probably know it, but tastelessness has never been far from the sense of fun at the core of rock and roll, or bombast either, these days. Back in the days when people spent a lot of time sitting stiff-backed in drawing rooms and there were no child labour laws, Mussorgsky wrote a piano chart called *Pictures At An Exhibition*, which was later rearranged for full orchestra by Maurice Ravel, whose smash hit *Bolero* was (comparatively) recently covered by Jeff Beck. *Pictures* is basically a series of short compositions meant to describe some paintings hanging in the Louvre, I believe, and back in the Kennedy sixties before I got my sensibilities corrupted

Why Pictures At An Exhibition?

and attention span obliterated by The Beatles et al, it was one of my fave classical raves. If poor old Mussorgsky and Ravel can hear what Emerson, Lake and Palmer have done to their music, they are probably getting dry heaves in the Void; speaking strictly as a fan of M & R and heretofore certified disdainer of EL&P, however, I can say that I listened to it twice tonight, beating my fists on the floor and laughing, and I got my kicks."

The review continued; "The proceedings, recorded live in England, begin with Mussorgsky's basic and conjunctive theme, the 'Promenade', played in a somewhat Bach-ic style, as if Keith Emerson were whacking away at the biggest pipe organ in the oldest church in Vienna. The 'Gnomes' theme from the original work, here credited to give such where it's due to (Mussorgsky/ Palmer), enters abruptly to whistles and yells from the audience, swizzled out on Emerson's Mellotron or customised organ or whatever, with wah-wah counterpoint by Lake. After some strange, kinetic soloing, 'Promenade' returns with lyrics by Lake: 'Lead me from tortured dreams...'. You said it, brother. Because from this point I begin to lose track of Mussorgsky and get caught up in the ELP furore for the rest of the side. Beginning with a Lake compo called 'The Sage' that has about as much to do with *Pictures At An Exhibition* as ELP's lyrics do with the programmatic significance of the original piece, but it's vintage ELP anyway, except for one boring bit where Lake indulges himself in some gossamer Laurindo Almeida-isms. Luckily, however, they don't last long. A minute later and we're hit in the face: Whizz! Whirrr! Whee! It's a full-blown slashing, crashing, urping, burping electronic freakout and boy does the crowd eat it up, along with the 'Blues Variation' which follows and takes the side out in gales of applause and more space bleeps. But what's this? I look in the album jacket and I see one of Mussorgsky's original themes, 'The Old Castle', listed (and supposedly elaborated on a bit by Emerson). Well, he must have elaborated the thing clear to Aldebaran, because I hear nary a hint of 'The Old Castle' anywhere on this record. Come to think of it, the original piece also had a couple of sections called 'Tuileries' and 'Ballet Of Chicks In Their Shells' (a sexist fantasy about a

ELP - *Pictures At An Exhibition*: In-depth

troupe of danseuses vacationing at the Black Sea being devoured by giant clams) that aren't even mentioned here. Oh well, fuck it, ELP know what they're doing and there's no sense having any dross cluttering up an otherwise fine album."

Also from the same review; "Side two begins with the 'Promenade' rendered stately as hell, heavy on the bass drum. They could play it at your high school graduation. Followed by a chart scripted by Mussorgsky completely without Limey and this time, called 'The Hut Of Baba Yaga', which in the original was about an old witch who went around snatching children and parboiling them for supper or some such. With such meaty subject matter, it stands to reason that it's done pretty much straight (except for the wah-wah Mellotron farts). Segueing into an ELP song called 'The Curse Of Baba Yaga' which for once seems to have some relation to Mussorgsky's themes, with a quick vocal that's almost impossible to catch and even quicker riffing — Keith Emerson really does know his axe inside and out, the Alvin Lee of Bach Rock — surging back through the original 'Baba Yaga' theme and right up to 'The Great Gates Of Kiev'. And man, when those gates open you better have some waterwings, 'cause the whole grand sprawling mess that's Emerson, Lake and Palmer at their best comes gushing out: not only a reprise of Whizz! and Whirrr!, but also Boink!, Grrr!, Skizzrrlll!, feedback and applause falling together like the walls of the Red Sea right after Moses' troops tramped through, and, yep, more lyrics: 'They were sent from the gate... For life to be...' Be what? He leaves the line to trail off in the air. The tension is unbearable, and the audience is fairly seething. But suddenly, abruptly, we are treated to the coda vocal and it all comes clear, sort of: 'There's no end to my life... Death is life'. Hmmm, don't know if I like them lines, sounds kinda like Charles Manson to me. But don't let the seeming obscurity fool you, because that inference is part of the grand plan too: the encore is 'Nut Rocker'."

Did Bangs really need to negate the merits of Jon Lord's *Gemini Suite* and *Concerto For Group And Orchestra* when reviewing ELP's *Pictures At An Exhibition*? I think not! Both

Why *Pictures At An Exhibition*?

pieces stand as artistically worthwhile in their own right. Similarly, both ELP's *Pictures* and Deep Purple's *Concerto* stand as monumental landmarks in the careers of both bands; they are both live recordings that would be all too easy to overlook in both band's discographies but actually, they were both important parts of both band's careers (even if they are more niche than, for instance, the studio albums *Tarkus* and *Deep Purple In Rock*). I advocate that one of the most agreeable things that Bangs mentions in his review of *Pictures At An Exhibition* is that, for anyone not tremendously familiar with Mussorgsky's original piece, it is very easy to listen to ELP's version and not be absolutely certain of who composed which bits. It is testament to the quality of ELP's writing as in, they succeeded to continue the mood and character of the original piece into something that they made their own. Although, it shouldn't come as a surprise really in terms of how both Emerson and Lake had always used classical music as a strong point of reference earlier in their careers.

By the time *Pictures At An Exhibition* was released, ELP's albums were an interesting mixture of character and musical direction. Their first album set the scene in terms of their overall sound. *Tarkus* was strongly linked around a concept and story. *Pictures At An Exhibition* was something of an anomaly because it wasn't a studio album and it wasn't an entirely original piece. Of course, ELP made Mussorgsky's piece very much their own, but still, it was an interesting choice of third album. So much so that even the band themselves often advocated that it was more of a sideline than their actual third album. However, The success of the *Pictures At An Exhibition* LP was such that next to *Tarkus*, in just six months ELP had managed to release two top three charting albums.

Chapter Two

The Making Of Pictures At An Exhibition

ELP's first tour spanned from September 1970 to March 1971. It included dates in the UK and Europe (see the full list in the appendix). Their performance of *Pictures At An Exhibition* at the Lyceum Theatre in London was filmed on the 9th December 1970. It was during a small break in the tour schedule in January 1971 that ELP went to Advision studios to record what would be released as their second album, *Tarkus*. The album's title track occupies side one of the LP. Released in June 1971, *Tarkus* got to number one in the UK and number nine in the US. After the UK and Europe, ELP began their first tour of North America on 24th April 1971 at Thiel College in Greenville, Pennsylvania. The tour continued through to late May and the rest of the year was occupied with more dates in Europe.

Lake was quoted in *Disc & Music Echo* in July 1971; "It took six days to record *Tarkus*. I don't know whether that's because there are so few people in the band, but I'm sure that doing an album quickly helps to make it sound fresh. If you spend four days on one song you lose a lot, whereas you can maintain one hundred percent energy if you only do it for a day. There is a danger in becoming analytical. In some ways you score but in others you dip badly. If you take out a note because it's slightly flat you lose the rawness and aggression."

Tarkus was reviewed in the *Reading Evening Post* in June 1971; "I honestly can't make head nor tail of this one. It would seem to be about some futuristic armadillo who has tank tracks and guns sprouting out of his sides. From what I can make out from the inside of the cover, this boyo spends his time trolling about having battles with equally futuristic animals. Side one is taken up with the musical story of Tarkus. A lot of it is conducted at a fast-and-furious pace, with Carl Palmer laying the beat thick, heavy and intricately. Keith Emerson, rightly acknowledged as one of the top organists around at the moment, puts in some descriptive passages — particularly in 'Eruption' and 'Aquatarkus', the beginning and the end of the piece. While I say I can't really understand what it's all about, I do understand one thing — it's darn good rock. The other side is up to the same standard, particularly the last track, a happy rocker called 'Are You Ready, Eddy?', which is dedicated to the sound engineer."

To be completely honest, transcribing this review cracked me up something chronic. The reviewer has really gone to great lengths to personify this *Tarkus* character! Still though, Carl Palmer was quoted in *Record Collector* in February 2014; "It was given to us on a storyboard. When we realised this thing (the mutant armadillo) was going back to the sea to lay some eggs, we said, 'We need aqua-type music; what are we going to do?' It wasn't a particularly well thought-out story; a bit childlike. It wasn't a mature concept like *The Dark Side Of The Moon* or *The Wall* — and Pink Floyd was a lot bigger than ELP. But we did start off that conceptual prog approach."

Tarkus was reviewed in the *Thanet Times* in June 1971: "The new single releases are looking totally uninspiring this week, so this space will be dedicated to reviewing the month's best albums. And with Emerson, Lake and Palmer topping the bill, who needs singles? The inimitable ELP's second album is now in the shops and many of their fans are likely to want a taste of their smooth harmonies and Moog synthesiser. Yes *Tarkus* — that monster from the unknown so beloved to Keith, Carl and Greg — is bound to be a monster success. The activities of Tarkus take up the whole of side one and is a feature of their live dates. Back in April, Thanet ELP followers were treated to the creature's fiery escapades at Margate's Winter Gardens. And if the one thousand plus audience's response to the group's performance is anything to go

ELP - *Pictures At An Exhibition*: In-depth

by, this album will soon be in the possession of every one of those fans. The imagination runs riot as this side spins, the intermittent squeals of the Moog adding to the incredible atmosphere conjured up. Then it's back to reality on side two, where some good old rock and roll in the form of 'Are You Ready, Eddy?' brings us back to our senses. This track is a tribute to Eddie Offord, their engineer. On to more lighter sounds and it's 'Jeremy Bender', during which Keith excels on piano."

It was reported in *Disc & Music Echo* in July 1971; "As far as this year is concerned Emerson, Lake and Palmer could be the hardest working band. They've done around one hundred concerts (each at least two hours long) in about one hundred and fifty days. Now their second album, *Tarkus* is top in Britain, and success hasn't come by way of self-indulgence or ignoring the need to entertain audiences. If you like, ELP are 'un-cool'. They know exactly what they are going to play when they go on stage, and they put themselves into it. It's not strictly a policy, but they are doing things the way they feel they ought to be done."

Palmer was quoted in *Beat Instrumental* in January 1971; "We've done twenty gigs since we started this band. Eighteen complete utter blinders — chairs broken, seats ripped, banned from halls, the lot! One gig, we were tired and only played half a blinder. The other was a bit under-the-arm, due to roadies."

Tarkus was reviewed in the *Newcastle Journal* in June 1971; "Thousands of Emerson, Lake and Palmer enthusiasts have already given their approval to the trio's second album, *Tarkus*. It was released only two weeks ago but is high in the LP charts and still rising. The achievement of the album is contained almost entirely on the first side, which shows Emerson at his majestic best making amazing use of his Moog synthesiser and Hammond Organ. After this sort of musical grandeur, the second side is a curious anti-climax, with the exception of where Emerson plays the organ of St Mark's Church, London, for a Bach toccata."

It was reported in *Disc & Music Echo* in July 1971; "So ELP are a straightforward, hardworking band. And they need to be. They have another US six-week tour lined up, starting at the

The Making Of Pictures At An Exhibition

Hollywood Bowl. They plan to make their third album in October and November, then there's another American tour, including Madison Square Gardens. And then there's a British twelve-day Christmas tour. You might think, after such hard work, and more to come, that Greg would be glad of the chance of a holiday. His management are even thinking of enlisting 'the aid of some heavies from Fulham to enforce a rest'."

Lake was quoted in the same feature; "But I've got so much to do. I'm recording an album for a group from Bournemouth, where my parents live." Greg Lake was working as the producer for a band called Spontaneous Combustion. He was quoted of them; "They have the same quality, tightness, and they're punchy. They do a lot of three-part harmony things but they are not like Yes musically. And Yes, by the way, like The Who, are one of the bands who give the music business energy and keep it alive. And there aren't many of them! Put that in: Yes always say nice things about us in interviews."

ELP's *Pictures At An Exhibition* album was released in the UK in November 1971. It features their performance that was recorded at Newcastle City Hall on 26th March 1971.

One eyewitness posted about the gig on the Internet on the Steve Hoffman Forum in March 2013 under the pseudonym of Rob Pieroni:

"I was at the gig, still live locally. ELP played the City Hall and Keith played the Hall's pipe organ on 'Pictures' on the UK tour previous to March '71, so they knew what they could expect when planning a live recording. The 'sssshh' from the audience at the start of the album was the general reaction to Greg saying 'we're recording tonight so please be quiet for the first part'; the organ was mic'd from the centre of the hall so it was always going to pick up anything ambient. I think we did okay. I'd love to hear again the rest of the gig, it was to the same quality of playing and if Mr Offord was recording should have been as well taped. The Hall historically has had a good acoustic track record, there's a couple of live tracks on the Small Faces *Autumn Stone* album."

"I'd dispute that the audience sound has been doctored but

ELP - *Pictures At An Exhibition*: In-depth

admit I am puzzled that all CD reissues so far haven't sonically joined up sides one and two of the vinyl. That much doesn't gel. I wrote the set list out onto my programme that evening thus:"

The Barbarian
Tarkus (I wrote 'Tarkas', it wasn't released at that date, bloomin' southern accents)
Jeremy Bender
Knife-Edge
Pictures At An Exhibition
Take A Pebble (piano improvs included 2nd Bridge from The Five Bridges Suite)
Rondo
Nut Rocker (encore)

Although the album is essentially just *Pictures At An Exhibition* it includes the encore of 'Nut Rocker'. There was much uncertainty regarding how the recording should be released, if at all! There was initially an idea to release *Pictures At An Exhibition* as the second ELP album following the success of their eponymous debut album. However, it was felt that the length and classical nature of the piece was such that it would struggle to get radio play. There was also a feeling from ELP that to release *Pictures At An Exhibition* as their second album would be a risk to their reputation overall because they didn't want to be pigeonholed as a band whose main thing was classical music. They decided to focus on *Tarkus* as their choice of second album.

It is very plausible that the success of *Tarkus* gave all concerned the confidence to release *Pictures At An Exhibition* as an album in its own right. When considering the beauty of *Pictures At An Exhibition*, there is arguably a poignancy to the thought that it perhaps took the success of a different piece of work for it to be felt that *Pictures* would be a worthy and viable release. It is understandable though. ELP were still in a tentative phase at the time. It was advocated in *Beat Instrumental* in January 1971; "Some of the critics have already come round — backing a

The Making Of Pictures At An Exhibition

favourite, so to speak (it would be difficult to ignore the success of the first album). Others are openly on the defensive. What they all utterly fail to see is that their self-important prognostications are irrelevant. Emerson, Lake and Palmer are good enough to survive the pettiness, the backbiting and the spite... They should be around for a long time."

It seems that a rocky reception from the press went some of the way towards inspiring ELP's reluctance to release *Pictures At An Exhibition* as an album. Lake was quoted in *Melody Maker* in February 1971; "The worst thing was the Festival Hall concert. I mean, it was a great concert man. It was good, we knew it was good and really enjoyed it. But you read the reviews and wonder if it was really the same gig. Public response has been incredible. All through the last tour it was like a madhouse, the reception we got. It wasn't just the applause at the end, they were clapping during numbers. Yet the press, instead of being fair and saying 'okay, now what do people feel about this group?', they don't report, they express their own opinion. It was criticism of a very low level. Okay, there were a couple of good criticisms which were founded. First thing that comes to mind is *Pictures At An Exhibition*, which was a classical interpretation, very similar to the kind of thing The Nice used to do. You look at anything Keith used to do and it was somebody else's work he had interpreted. That was one mistake. It was not wrong for the band in that I personally enjoyed doing it, but it was wrong because it gave the press, the critics, a lever. It gave them a way to make comparisons. *Pictures* is being dropped now because we are creating material ourselves and there's no longer room for it. We are doing two hours now. Add this next album and we will be on for four hours. People like to hear the current album so what we'll probably do is drop *Pictures*, do the first album in the first half and the next in the second."

Thankfully, *Pictures* wasn't dropped, it was just put on hold in favour of *Tarkus*, at least for a while.

Palmer was quoted of *Tarkus* in *Hit Parader* in January 1972; "I prefer to think of it as being the first album that we cut as a

ELP - *Pictures At An Exhibition*: In-depth

band. We were so much together on those sessions and playing without any pressures whereas our first album was more or less a proving point to initially show what we were capable of doing. On *Tarkus* we did it."

Emerson was quoted in *Beetle* in February 1974; "*Tarkus* was like a testing ground for us, I think, mainly because of the time changes and key changes. I think it was a good start for us to get into doing something that was really experimental. To that extent it means a lot to me." Lake was quoted in *New Musical Express* in July 1972; "Personally, I've always felt *Tarkus* was our best album collectively and so does Carl, but everyone's entitled to an opinion."

Both their first album, *Emerson Lake and Palmer* (1970) and *Tarkus* (1971) were within the top five in the UK album charts. Lake was quoted in *Melody Maker* in February 1971; "The first album was a balance, but it was a balance of individuals. There was Keith and I — but this time it (*Tarkus*) is together. He has written for me and I have written for him. Breaking it down to basics I suppose you could say that the instrumental parts are Keith's and the songs are mine. The aim is to achieve a working balance where the output of each person is allowed freedom, yet the total gels as one music. In many bands it happens that one person is musically not satisfied. What we've achieved is very pleasing, very pleasing indeed. But we have no clue, none whatsoever, of the second side. We are due in the studio on Tuesday and we have nothing at all."

Tarkus was reviewed in *The Record Songbook* in August 1971; "Anything progressive is thought-provoking, even controversial, and Emerson Lake and Palmer's second album — *Tarkus* on Island ILPS 9155 — has created a wide diversity of opinion among critics and reviewers. But, devotees will come down on the side of greatness and rate *Tarkus* a natural progression from ELP's debut LP. If you listen to both albums this is made clear. The whole of side one is called 'Tarkus' and is one continuous track with themes running through it. One 'movement' merges easily into the next, and the pattern is established with Lake's songs joined by Emerson's central theme. If you look at the inside sleeve pictures of the tank-like armadillo you'll be able to see that the story is being followed in the music on the record. 'Battlefield' is the climax on side one and the theme seems to mingle with the song. Anti-war! Slow, dramatic, atmospheric and beautiful in parts. Brilliant ELP! 'Aquatarkus' ends the story with the armadillo walking out to sea. Emerson ends the side instrumentally as it began. Climatic and dramatic with the early theme apparent, ending with heavy discords and one final long chord. See this side as a complete suite, and you discover the excitement ELP intended. Side two is a set of different songs that have no connection at all with side one. 'The Only Way (Hymn)' on track three is the only classical Emerson on the record. He plays St Mark's Church organ and there is a very good song from Lake based on *Toccata in F* and *Prelude VI* (Bach). Notable piano and bass work on this. 'A Time And A Place' is incredible! Great Lake vocal on this fast raver, with good Hammond organ riff from Emerson. Palmer's drumming strong and to the point. Keith Emerson, Greg Lake and Carl Palmer have, in *Tarkus*, once again proved their undoubted superiority!"

It was reported in *Circus* in March 1972; "*Pictures At An Exhibition*, ELP's version of the Mussorgsky classic, was recorded before *Tarkus*, and until it received an incredible string of reviews there were no plans to release it in America."

In the 2016 released deluxe edition of ELP's *Pictures At An Exhibition*, Chris Welch quoted Lake; "We took the recording to Atlantic and they didn't want to release it in the US. They said it didn't constitute a band album because it wasn't recorded in a studio and it wasn't classical music. They said, 'How are you going to get that on the radio?' We were signed to Island in England and label boss Chris Blackwell started to export records of *Pictures At An Exhibition* into America. Something like 120,000 copies sold in the first two weeks. Of course, Armet Ertegun saw this happening and said 'okay lads, you can have it out on our Atlantic label.' It even got played on WNEW by Scott Mooney in New York, the first time the whole side of an album was played on radio. The phone lines lit up and it caused a sensation."

The reporter advocated of *Pictures At An Exhibition* in *Beetle*

ELP - *Pictures At An Exhibition*: In-depth

in February 1974; "In fact, it was the first thing Emerson, Lake and Palmer ever played together. Gradually the fun turned to sourness and they delayed releasing it for quite some time. When it did come out, it was looked upon by a lot of people as a landmark in rock when in a lot of ways it was an immense disappointment."

Emerson was quoted in the same feature; "We had our first album out. When we first went out on the road we were doing *Pictures At An Exhibition*. When we first started playing to new audiences there was that similarity between ELP and The Nice: 'Oh. It's just the 'New' Nice'. We got very dejected by this, and we thought that possibly the reason people were thinking this was because we were doing adaptations of classical music and people really got carried away by this. They thought that was all we were doing, that was our only output. We were the band that did classical music: we knew they had got it wrong because we were writing our own pieces of music. We didn't want to release *Pictures At An Exhibition* mainly because we knew what people were going to say about it ('it looks like it's the old Nice, they're doing classical music'). Also, it would have taken up a whole album and left us no room to do anything of our own, so we purposely delayed it. We purposely put *Tarkus* out as a second album to show that we could write our own things, and to try to let the whole classical thing die away. When we did release it, we released it at a reduced price, as if to say 'get rid of it'. There was a big demand for it, so we brought it out. We recorded it live, somewhere in Newcastle and we just sort of got it out of the way. Sure enough, they did the bit there."

Greg Lake explained in his autobiography; "There was talk of releasing the Newcastle City Hall recording as ELP's second album, but the record company was not convinced that an interpretation of a whole classical suite was going to sell, despite how it had gone down at our live performances. The idea was shelved for the time being, but after the success of our second album and tour, it was released in November 1971, reaching number three in the UK album charts. As well as *Pictures*, the album included the live encore of 'Nut Rocker', inspired by Kim Fowley's version of the

The Making Of Pictures At An Exhibition

March from Tchaikovsky's ballet, *The Nutcracker*." The performance of *Pictures At An Exhibition* recorded at Newcastle City Hall opens with Emerson playing the venue's pipe organ. Installed in 1928, it was positioned a considerable distance above stage level. As a result, Palmer played a drum roll that was long enough to cover the amount of time Emerson needed to get back down to the stage for playing the next part of the piece.

Newcastle City Hall was opened in 1927. It was built as part of a development plan that included the City Pool. Over the years, it has been a popular venue for orchestras, bands, stand up comedy and social gatherings. Many high-profile bands have performed at Newcastle City Hall over the years and ELP are part of a strong legacy in such regard. The Animals played there in 1968, Lindisfarne played there in July 1970 and The Byrds played there in May 1971. Wishbone Ash recorded tracks for an album, *Live Dates* in June 1973. Roxy Music recorded tracks for *Viva! Roxy Music* in October 1974. In 1981 Motörhead used the venue for recording some of the tracks on their live album, *No Sleep 'til Hammersmith*. In the same year, Slade performed and recorded a performance that was released as an album titled *Slade On Stage*.

Along with the thought that went into setting up prior to the performance of *Pictures At An Exhibition*, Newcastle City Hall must have been a good choice of venue for acoustics. It was considered in *Circus* in March 1972; "One of the things the critics have praised most about the *Pictures* album is the sound quality; this is no accident. Poor reproduction is one of the major hazards of recording live."

Emerson was quoted in the same feature; "It's not easy to get a good sound. When we recorded *Pictures* in England, we spent all day just working on the sound system... *Pictures At An Exhibition* was recorded live because it contained a lot of improvisation. I get more of a buzz playing an improvisation live than playing it cold in the studio. I probably will do more live recording, it just takes a lot to get it together."

Really, ELP's performance at Newcastle City Hall did positive things for Newcastle; it got the county and the venue some good

ELP - *Pictures At An Exhibition*: In-depth

publicity. It was reported in the *Newcastle Evening Chronicle* in December 1971; "A new pop LP could make Newcastle City Hall an internationally known name. The record is Emerson, Lake and Palmer's interpretation of Mussorgsky's *Pictures At An Exhibition*. And it was recorded during a concert at the City Hall. It is the first time the City Hall has been used for an issued recording, except for the occasional television or radio programme, and hall manager Mr Bob Brown is delighted with the result. One critic on a weekly music paper praises 'the brilliance of the hall's acoustics.' More people 'should record live at Newcastle City Hall,' he adds, 'the sound is incredible.' Mr Brown says: 'This record is absolutely fantastic. It should kill the myth that the acoustics in the City Hall are bad. It is time we stopped getting knocking reviews, and people realise what the hall has to offer. I couldn't be more pleased.' The LP is expected to sell more than a million copies, through sales on the continent, in the United States and Japan. Emerson, Lake and Palmer records are regularly high in the British LP charts. The group developed from The Nice which starred Geordie bass player Lee Jackson — and which split up after recording a tribute to Newcastle, 'The Five Bridges Suite'. Emerson, Lake and Palmer achieve an orchestra sound with an electronic keyboard instrument called a Moog synthesiser. The group closes its performance with 'Nut Rocker', another popped-up classic based on Tchaikovsky's *Nutcracker* suite. Bob Brown says there are further plans for recording pop music at the City Hall. 'Both Tyne Tees and BBC TV are recording the Newcastle group Lindisfarne for documentaries', he said."

ELP were made very welcome in Newcastle. In the 2016 liner notes of ELP's *Pictures At An Exhibition*, Chris Welch quoted Emerson; "We had a strong following in Newcastle, maybe because my old friend Lee Jackson of The Nice came from there and we'd recorded the Nice's 'Five Bridges Suite' in the city's honour. The audience was very respectful and listening attentively while Greg was singing the quiet passages. But if they had shouted, it might have made me less nervous! I can't stand quiet audiences."

Compared to the size of crowds that ELP were used to

performing for, the seat capacity at Newcastle City Hall is relatively small; it comes in at just over two thousand in total. Lake was quoted in *Crawdaddy* in August 1971; "Sometimes I can play better to a small audience than to a big audience."

Emerson was quoted in *The New York Times* in December 1973; "It is very hard to get something across to 10,000 people with just a piano, a bass and a set of drums. It works fine in smaller places and in the recording studio — I always compose first on the piano — but in the large arenas where we have to play, everything gets lost... We are programmed to write for the big audience and that is why we have and need the big equipment. It isn't all for show."

Greg Lake recalled; "Having recorded our second album, the band had really begun to find its feet and we had more than enough material to draw upon in order to keep the shows fresh and vibrant. The UK dates were mainly the usual city halls and so on but, despite being relatively small, these were fantastic places to perform in — it was in those time-honoured venues that we really began to develop the whole theatrical concept of the band's performance. Even though all of those city hall shows were great to play, the most memorable one on that particular tour was at Newcastle City Hall on 26th March 1971 when we recorded our live adaptation of Mussorgsky's *Pictures At An Exhibition*. Keith played the opening 'Promenade' section on an old Harrison & Harrison organ permanently installed above the stage in the hall."

Not all of the venues that ELP played at were considered suitable. Whilst people were keen to welcome the band to play at Margate's Winter Gardens, it later emerged that they wouldn't feel happy to return. It was reported in the *Thanet Times* in March 1971; "Later this month Margate's Winter Gardens will be throbbing to the best of three British rock musicians of the highest order — the electrifying Emerson, Lake and Palmer, in concert. The group will be performing non-stop for three hours on Monday 29th March, with absolutely no breaks and no supporting group. Margate Entertainment Manager, Mr Jack Green, told me: 'Already the ground floor is heavily booked. News of the

ELP - *Pictures At An Exhibition*: In-depth

concert has been announced in the pop papers, *Melody Maker* and *New Musical Express*. As a result, we have been inundated with applications for seats.' He added that the booking of ELP had only just been arranged and that followers of the group — who will undoubtedly not only come from Thanet — are likely to make the evening a memorable one. Keith Emerson joined forces with Greg Lake and Carl Palmer nine months ago, creating an outcry from the many who thought they would be 'top of the flops'. But Emerson (ex-Nice), Lake (ex-King Crimson) and Palmer (former drummer with Arthur Brown's Crazy World) soon silenced the critics by becoming one of the country's most rapid and authentic supergroups. One of their albums, entitled *Emerson, Lake and Palmer*, smashed into the LP charts and soared to the dizzy heights of number two in no time at all. No doubt tracks from their future album, *Tarkus*, will abound at the Winter Gardens concert. And one song they will almost certainly perform is 'Nut Rocker'. They will, I am told, probably ask people on this tour, whether they think it should be included on the album. Keith is a fine exponent of the keyboard, Greg excels as a vocalist/writer/guitarist and Carl's drumming is really something else. One feature of their music is excessive use of the Moog synthesiser. A fine example of this is on their record 'Lucky Man' which is currently being spun on all the best disc jockeys' turntables. Each full sounding record is deserving of a number one in the charts without the preliminaries of first being a climber... The performance starts at 7:30pm and I am sure if the audience had their way it would never end."

Following the concert, the following month the same paper reported: "The Winter Gardens at Margate — scene from a recent pop concert by top rock band, Emerson, Lake and Palmer — is being snubbed as a future venue for similar gigs on the grounds of being 'unsuitable'. John and Tony Smith Entertainments, who as well as staging the ELP concert also handled the bookings on the recent Rolling Stones tour, have scrapped their plans to hold another concert at the Winter Gardens next month. Before the start of the ELP gig last Monday, a spokesman for John and Tony said they were planning to bring down underground heroes T.

The Making Of Pictures At An Exhibition

Rex to the same venue on 10th May, and, later on, King Crimson. But when I contacted John Smith at his Reigate, Surrey-based organisation, he said 'we are not going to do it'. He added, 'The Winter Gardens is just not suitable because the lighting and the whole setup of the hall is bad. ELP, he said, left Margate after their concert — which met with frenzied and often hysterical response from a one thousand plus audience — unhappy with the décor and the whole scene. Guitarist/vocalist Greg Lake unknowingly backed up this comment after the concert when, quenching his thirst from a bottle of water, he said: 'The audience were far too quiet.' Continued John: 'It did not produce the right atmosphere. And if you don't have many concerts of a high standard in Thanet, that is probably why.' Tony Smith, who said 'the Winter Gardens is not the best concert hall in the world', added that although they would still like T. Rex to perform in Thanet, it now seemed to be out of the question. A spokesman for the Winter Gardens said at the weekend: 'We have been told that the audience was not up to what it could have been, but I thought it was reasonably good. They also made a comment about the lighting being bad. This surprises me because they thought after last week's concert that the hall was very good. In fact, they congratulated us on it'."

There is an element of "he said, she said" in the report as in, it is not particularly clear as to who it was that made the conclusive decision to withdraw further interest in performing at the Winter Gardens. Whether the decision was made by ELP or management though, the report is demonstrative of the fact that a lot of thought went into which venues would best provide ELP with the scope to feel that they were giving their best.

It's ironic really; surely it should be an audience who decides if they want to welcome a band back, rather than the other way round?! In such regard, it is understandable as to how some may have perceived ELP as being pretentious. But then again, if an element of perfection is at play, or at least the need to feel confident in every possible element of performing live then the position taken by the band and/or their management is certainly understandable. With it being the case that ELP put thought into

ELP - *Pictures At An Exhibition*: In-depth

where they were happy to play live, it highlights the thought that must have gone into making Newcastle City Hall the location of choice for the recording of *Pictures At An Exhibition*.

This was also a time in rock where a percentage of the predominantly male audiences not only delved into the music in detail, but also the instrumentation that made it. This technical stuff isn't for everyone but I'm including it because it will be of interest to some and it shows the scale of thought that ELP put into the technical aspect of their performance.

In January 1971 in *Melody Maker* it was asked what equipment Lake uses on stage. He answered the question as follows: "I play a Gibson JT100 custom guitar which costs £600 and is the model used by Elvis Presley. It is miked through the PA via an AKG condenser microphone and I use Darco strings, which are made in America. My bass guitar is a Fender Jazz Bass, with Rotosound wire-woundstrings. It goes through two 200-watt Hiwatt amps. I have four tuned Hiwatt cabinets containing 1,600 watts of bass speakers. I also have a fuzz and wah-wah on the bass, which are operated by foot pedals. Our PA is a WEM consisting of 2,000 watts of speakers driven by two Crown stereo amplifiers. There are four Loudmouth stacks, 16 4x12, 7 6x10 and 4 Tannoy cabinets. We have a 20-channel stereo mixer."

It was reported in *Beat Instrumental* in January 1971; "Emerson uses a grand piano, a Moog synthesiser, an electric Clavinet, and two Hammonds — one a brand new A100 and the other his tried and trusty — though battered — L100 for stunting purposes. Greg Lake alternates between his Fender bass and his massive Gibson Jumbo for acoustic work. Carl, surrounded by drums, has two enormous gongs either side of him."

It wasn't made clear in either account as to whether the latter set of equipment was used during the recording of *Pictures At An Exhibition* but either way, the lists are demonstrative of where ELP were at with things technically around that time and clearly, everyone in the group put a lot of care into setting up their kit before a performance. Emerson was quoted in *The New York Times* in December 1973; "I have to tune it all up and that takes

The Making Of Pictures At An Exhibition

about an hour before each concert."

The cover art for *Pictures At An Exhibition* was commissioned to the artist, William Neal. All of the frames on the front cover of the album contain blank canvases. It's not until the gatefold is opened that Neal's art can be seen. He designed and painted every picture that is featured on the gatefold sleeve — a total of seven. Prior to being scaled for use in the gatefold of the album, Neal made paintings that corresponded with each title in *Pictures*. They were large oil paintings, sometimes with imagery relating to ELP embedded in them. The background from *Tarkus* features in 'Hut'. Greg Lake's dog, Oliver, a red setter, was painted in 'The Sage'. Neal's paintings were exhibited at London's Hammersmith Town Hall. They were photographed by graduates from the Guildford School of Art, Keith Morris and Nigel Marlow.

Lake advocated; "William Neal, who created the *Tarkus* cover, did another great one for *Pictures At An Exhibition*, relating the idea of a gallery of paintings, blank on the outside but with the revealed artworks inside the gatefold." Neal did the cover art for *Tarkus* prior to doing it for *Pictures At An Exhibition*. 'Promenade' remains blank. Whilst the LP gatefold allowed for a sense of reveal in how Neal's art was presented, in recent years, some CD releases of *Pictures At An Exhibition* only feature the paintings on the front cover.

Also a graduate of the Guildford School of art, Neal had worked for the BBC, Ulster TV, Pitman Publishing and a design group in London's West End, CCS Associates. It was through the latter that he met Greg Lake. His work has also been used by other bands such as Stone The Crows, Audience, The Mick Abrahams Band and the Upsetters. Neal also provided art for members of ELP on their solo projects much later down the line. His painting, Moonlit Dunes, features on Keith Emerson's 2012 album, *Three Fates Project*. In 2013, one of Neal's original paintings for *Pictures At An Exhibition* featured on Carl Palmer album, *Working Live Vol. 3*.

It was advocated in *Circus* in March 1972; "One critic in England said that listening to a live record of Emerson, Lake and

ELP - *Pictures At An Exhibition*: In-depth

Palmer is even more satisfying than seeing them, because when you attend their concerts, too many visuals attract your attention and detract from the music."

The filmed version of ELP's *Pictures At An Exhibition* was met with a mixed reception. It was reported in the *Wishaw Press & Advertiser* in November 1972; "The exciting pop group — Emerson, Lake and Palmer — take to the big screen in a ninety-eight minute movie called *Pictures At An Exhibition*, their film which is of a live concert is supported by well known group Strawbs in *Grave New World* and The Scaffold in *Plod*. The group's masterly rendition of the Mussorgsky set is illustrated by a surprising, but somehow very appropriate, choice of images including those from Marvel Comics. Strawbs album *Grave New World* lasts for thirty minutes. The Scaffold's appearance at the Edinburgh Festival led to their movie *Plod*, the theme of which is The Scaffold's eccentric look at law and order in today's society."

Under the heading of "Russian Classic Goes Pop", the *Kensington Post* asserted in September 1972; "Mussorgsky's *Pictures At An Exhibition* gets a very special treatment by the pop group Emerson, Lake and Palmer in a ninety minute colour film using electronic devices such as visual feedback, signal generators and colour synthesisers. Producer Lindsey Clennell has developed a highly personal style which turns a simple documentary record of a concert into a fluid dynamic visualisation of the music itself. The sound quality is exceptional, with the eight-track recording supervised by Greg Lake to capture the vibrant quality of the group's performance without departing from their high recording standards. Their rendition of the Mussorgsky set is illustrated by a surprising, but somehow very appropriate, choice of images including those from Marvel Comics. The group is aiming for a place in music, not merely in rock 'n' roll. They have overcome the initial dilemma of individual musical forces finding a natural balance, and their identity is strong."

It was reported in the *Harrow Observer* in June 1973; "*Pictures At An Exhibition* with Emerson, Lake and Palmer is a film version of their concert at the Lyceum which included their

The Making Of Pictures At An Exhibition

version of Mussorgsky's work from where the film gets its title. As interpreted by the group, the classic piece, redefined in pop terms, takes on an improvisatory quality and their version is a superb piece of music in its own right."

The material that features on the film of *Pictures At An Exhibition* was recorded before the performance at Newcastle City Hall took place. Upon being asked whether *Pictures At An Exhibition* would be released on an album, Lake was quoted in *Melody Maker* in February 1971; "Well, we have had the tape made by the film people at the Lyceum concert. *Pictures* runs for forty minutes, and it cost us nothing to make. You see, we don't want to go back on it and re-record it because that's a phase and has gone. We played it last night, probably for the last time. But there are people who want it, so what we might do it put that in as a separate LP with the new album, and not make any extra charge for it."

Not everyone was happy with the filmed version, Lake included. He asserted in his autobiography; "A film of our performance of *Pictures At An Exhibition* at the Lyceum in London in November 1970 had been released but it was shockingly bad, both in terms of the filming and the sound quality and we wanted to redress the balance by releasing a proper live recording that would capture the energy of the band." It is possible that ELP may have wanted to downplay the film of *Pictures At An Exhibition* at the Lyceum due to the relative commercial failure of the cinema release.

In the 2016 release, Chris Welch explained in the liner notes; "CD1 features the complete and remastered twelve tracks from the original 1971 album, as recorded at Newcastle City Hall and released in December 1971. Also included are seven tracks from the band's performance of *Pictures* recorded at the Mar Y Sol Festival, Puero Rico in April 1972. On disc two we are treated to an earlier ELP performance of *Pictures* recorded and filmed at the Lyceum Theatre, London on December 9th 1970." I advocate that the deluxe edition of *Pictures At An Exhibition* is a worthwhile purchase on the basis that it presents an opportunity to hear the

ELP - *Pictures At An Exhibition*: In-depth

variations in the performance of the piece a well as the elements of it that they remained pretty much consistent with.

Chapter Three

How Does ELP's Version Compare To Mussorgsky's?

When I say "how do the two pieces compare?", it is not with the intention of wanting to elevate the status of one over and above the other. That would be futile. Mussorgsky's original composition and ELP's version of *Pictures At An Exhibition* are both beautiful pieces of music in their own right. Not only that but they are both very *relevant* pieces of music in their own right. Mussorgsky's piece has stood the test of time as a widely appreciated piece of classical music and ELP's version of it was a signature performance for the band as well as an interesting example of progressive rock. So when I say "how do the two pieces compare?" what I'm really getting at is "how were ELP faithful to Mussorgsky's original piece? What did they keep in, what did they omit and what did they add of their own?" This is an important question because it provides the scope with which it becomes possible to appreciate why ELP's version of *Pictures At An Exhibition* is distinctive in its own right.

Pictures At An Exhibition was reviewed in the *Reading Evening Post* in January 1972; "I have only recently become addicted to ELP and this record has got me hooked even further. It is the trio's interpretation of the classic suite by Mussorgsky. On first hearing I found myself comparing it unfavourably to the original, but you have to bear in mind that this is the young, modern interpretation. Really, ELP have taken over Mussorgsky's theme and woven their own characteristic sounds and style around it. Keith Emerson is, of course, faultless with his intricate

ELP - *Pictures At An Exhibition*: In-depth

keyboard work and once again he explores scores of sounds with his Moog. Carl Palmer is as heavy and as furious as ever, but the highlight for me was the quiet interlude with Greg on guitar and vocal in 'The Sage'. The album was recorded live at Newcastle City Hall and the reproduction is first class. This suite has been a highlight of the band's established act for a long time, so it could only really have been done before a crowd. This must be another hit for them."

Interestingly, the review draws attention to the fact that with *Pictures At An Exhibition*, not only was ELP's work going to be compared to their previous albums but also, to the original Mussorgsky piece. Whilst Emerson's playing of the main theme, 'Promenade', is melodically on point (faithful to the original) and indeed beautiful, thereafter, there is a lot to be said for listening to ELP's version as something in and of itself, rather than reaching frequently at how it perhaps compares to Mussorgsky's. Still though, that's the risk that any band takes when they do their own version of an exiting piece of music. Besides, it's still fascinating to compare the two pieces in terms of, what did ELP bring to the table?

The publishing history of Mussorgsky's *Pictures At An Exhibition* is a complicated one. Despite the speed at which he composed the piece, it didn't appear in print until 1886, five years after his death. It was Mussorgsky's friend and colleague, Nikolai Rimsky-Korsakov who prepared an edition of the score for publication but problematically, it was generally believed that this edition wasn't an accurate portrayal of Mussorgsky's original work. It wasn't until 1931 that *Pictures At An Exhibition* was published in agreement with his manuscript. Further to this, it wasn't until 1975 that Mussorgsky's actual manuscript was published in facsimile.

After having composed it, Mussorgsky was happy to leave *Pictures At An Exhibition* as the piano piece that he had intended it to be. It was Maurice Ravel's orchestral version of the piece that introduced it to a wider audience. There had been previous attempts at an orchestral arrangement, but it wasn't until 1922

How Does ELP's Version Compare To Mussorgsky's?

that Ravel finished what became recognised as the well-known version.

Mussorgsky's composition is based on paintings by the artist Viktor Hartmann. He was also an architect and a designer. A friend of Hartmann's, Mussorgsky was deeply affected by his death on 4th August 1873, so much so that he was inspired to compose the piece that came to be titled *Pictures At An Exhibition*. Mussorgsky originally composed it for piano and finished his score in a matter of just three weeks in June 1874.

The music depicts an exhibition of Hartmann's artwork. Each number in Mussorgsky's suite is a musical portrayal of a Hartman painting. Hartmann's art was largely based on his travels to other parts of Europe; France, Italy, Ukraine and Poland. Sadly, the majority of the paintings are now lost and as a result, it isn't possible to ascertain which exact works of art Mussorgsky was referring to when he composed each section of *Pictures At An Exhibition*. Nevertheless, each section is named in a way that is, at least to some extent, suggestive of the content of each painting. The structure of Mussorgsky's *Pictures At An Exhibition* is as follows:

Promenade
1. The Gnome
Promenade
2. The Old Castle
Promenade
3. Tuileries (Children's Quarrel After Games)
4. Cattle
Promenade
5. Ballet Of Unhatched Chicks
6. "Samuel" Goldenberg and "Schmuÿle"
Promenade
7. Limoges. The Market (The Great News)
8. Catacombs (Roman Tomb)
    With The Dead An A Dead Language
9. The Hut On Hen's Legs (Baba Yaga)
10. The Great Gates Of Kiev

ELP - *Pictures At An Exhibition*: In-depth

As I'll get onto later in this chapter, ELP's version of *Pictures At An Exhibition* makes a lot of reference to Baba Yaga so at this point, it's time to clarify who/what that actually means. Well, in the context of Slavic folklore, Baba Yaga is a supernatural being (sometimes regarded as a trio of three sisters, sometimes described as just one being). She is a scary looking old woman who, in Russian fairytales, flies around in a mortar whilst wielding a pestle. She lives in a hut in the forest and has the power to either help or harm. Which of those two things she does is often left as ambiguous. Skinny and with long chicken legs, with iron teeth and a long nose, this frightening character lives in a hut that legend says is surrounded by a fence made of human bones (so if any of the Baba Yaga bits in either Mussorgsky's or ELP's version of *Pictures At An Exhibition* strike you as somewhat chilling or spooky, there was probably method in the madness when it came to composing with Baba Yaga in mind).

ELP's version of *Pictures At An Exhibition* contains eleven movements and they all vary with regards to the extent that they were loyal to Mussorgsky's original composition. In some cases, ELP is very faithful to the original, in others they are a bit freer with it and there are also movements that are the band's own composition entirely. Emerson was quoted in *Crawdaddy* in August 1971; "Usually an arrangement starts off with one idea, a positive conception of a piece... Then arrangement is really interpretation on your part — the individual's part. And the way I might interpret affects the way he plays his part. An arrangement sort of grows like that: a really tight arrangement is worked on as you go."

In choosing to embrace classical music influences, there was also a sense of ELP wanting to remain true to their heritage rather than drawing inspiration from what was in vogue at the time. Emerson was quoted in *Q Magazine* in 1992; "I've mentioned this before, but whereas a lot of bands from our generation developed their style from black blues, what we wanted to do when we got together in 1970 was stick to our heritage. We're white, we're European, we didn't want to pretend to be something that we're

How Does ELP's Version Compare To Mussorgsky's?

not." Such approach was noticed by the media at the time. It was advocated of ELP in *The New York Times* in December 1973; "Like Procol Harum, Soft Machine, Focus, Genesis and even the Moody Blues, they have evolved a distinctly European brand of rock, rejecting the conventional soul-blues approach."

And of course, referring to classical music wasn't unfamiliar terrain. Greg Lake recalled in his autobiography; "By the time King Crimson and The Nice were playing on the same bill in the States, the Nice's set list would include reworkings of some Bob Dylan songs together with versions of Bach and Tchaikovsky pieces. Meanwhile King Crimson were mixing together Holst's *The Planets*, quite heavy rock, jazz and folk, and the two bands together were spearheading what would become the progressive rock scene."

In some ways, it could be said that doing their own interpretation of a classical piece of music made absolute sense for ELP in terms of how they worked. Working to something structured and established was held in higher regard than jamming. Lake was quoted in *Disc & Music Echo* in July 1971; "We don't spend hours jamming, none of that nonsense. What we do is ninety percent arranged, musically. That's the way all of us feel and that's the way it works out. I can't stand bands who spend hours tuning up with fags hanging out their mouths, with their backs to the audience, and then jam for four hours on a twelve-bar. It doesn't happen for me. We're conscious of giving an audience entertainment. That's why I admire The Who. Apart from their musical quality, they get stuck in and always give a good two-to-two-and-a-half-hour performance. There are a lot of moodies around and it used to be profitable to be a moody, but I never got into that, and I don't think it pays any more."

Equally though, ELP weren't aloof when it came to engaging an audience. Lake was quoted in *Gig* in September 1977; "I'm sure if someone screamed 'boogie' in the middle of the piano concerto, Keith would probably break into a quick twelve bar to keep them amused, cast a sly glance in their direction and continue. We're not beyond a sense of humour."

ELP - *Pictures At An Exhibition*: In-depth

Lake was quoted in *The Daily Mirror* in October 1972; "One of the most difficult periods of my life was earlier this year when I realised all of a sudden we had nobody to compete with. The three of us are good and the group is better than any of us. But I've learned that every door you walk through, there's always another door. And baby, you've got to keep pushing." Admittedly, I am cautious to put this quote out there because it could be considered that Lake's comment was somewhat crass or arrogant. However, by late 1972, ELP had achieved so much in such a relatively short space of time and if having a strong sense of self belief in what they were doing fuelled that, then well, fair enough really.

Lake was quoted in *New Musical Express* in November 1973; "I know people think we're pretentious, but it's really a product of sophistication. All I can say is that we love what we play and what we write. We don't do it to impress people. But on the other hand our music and lyrics aren't instant things. You can't pick them up without putting some work into it, and anything that makes demands on the listener could be called pretentious. Some people don't want to put any work into it — which is alright. Maybe they don't like music that much, and there's nothing wrong with that — but those who are really into it want something more satisfying. To judge pretentiousness I think you must look at the people behind it and their motives. As a band we're trying to advance our instruments — sometimes to a bizarre degree — which obviously puts some people off. But we're only trying to give pleasure. We just want to do something that'll surprise people, entertain them or maybe even shock them. That's all it is. I agree we're not going to get respect by letting off a couple of cannons but it might startle a few people. Y'see, we've always wanted to extend the band. From the start we wanted to avoid being a sort of band in jeans with no show and pretending to be the same as the kids down there. I don't think any audience wants to see that… I mean, if you look at a painter, he's usually a different kind of guy from the cat who buys his pictures. That's what artists have always been through the ages — a bit freaky, a bit bizarre, but also entertaining. The same thing applies to rock musicians, and that's what the public

How Does ELP's Version Compare To Mussorgsky's?

wants them to be."

In particular, it is likely that *Pictures At An Exhibition* lent itself well to ELP's writing style on the basis of all the imagery that was already there in Mussorgsky's composition. Lake was quoted in *Disc & Music Echo* in July 1971; "Sometimes the music suggests something visual, sometimes a word pattern. I think our material always has a strong melody, or a tangible form. Music that doesn't have a tangible form is always the hardest to write lyrics for because you need a tremendous amount of imagination."

In terms of what inspires him musically, Lake was quoted in *New Musical Express* in November 1973; "It comes out of a love for writing things, a love of imagining things, imagining a form and making it concrete. A lot of art comes out of difficulty, a lot out of rebellion. For me it's imagination."

Upon being asked why out of all the classical pieces of music, he chose to do a full blown adaptation of *Pictures At An Exhibition*, Emerson was quoted in *Beetle* in February 1974; "I liked it. I just liked the tune and I wanted to play it. It's as simple as that. I have a love for classical music and I like jazz as well. There aren't many rock bands I listen to. I spend about six months writing a piece of music of my own. So it's kind of refreshing to me to play something else written by someone else, something which I like. I first heard *Pictures At An Exhibition* at the Royal Festival Hall performed by an orchestra and I came out of the concert thinking it was far out, I've got to play that."

And back at the same venue, as was considered in *Beat Instrumental* in January 1971, "From the moment they walked onstage, the sell-out audience was in the palms of their hands. Keith played the first bars of *Pictures At An Exhibition* on the Festival Hall organ and it was total jubilation right through to the second encore. The more one reflects on the sheer visual brilliance of Emerson, Lake and Palmer on stage, the more it becomes impossible to avoid the impression that earlier criticisms were based on spite rather than objectivity."

It was advocated in the *Reading Evening Post* in June 1971; "I reckon some pop compositions could end up as classics in their

ELP - *Pictures At An Exhibition*: In-depth

own right — pieces like *Tarkus* by Emerson, Lake and Palmer, for instance." In the same feature, the journalist commented in a general sense and without regard to any particular group, "I'm all for exploration and innovation but this sort of thing is neither: it seems to me that writers are trying to produce an 'important' piece by saying it is classical or symphonic or what have you. And it is not important or even impressive. Far from it in fact."

It's interesting that certainly, a lot of people had the propensity to perhaps be more welcoming of *Tarkus* than *Pictures At An Exhibition* — purely on the basis that when something is considered to be under the umbrella of classical music, that alone can be enough to put some listeners off. But of course, ELP went beyond the scope of classical music in terms of what they did with Mussorgsky's piece.

ELP's version of *Pictures At An Exhibition*, in addition the famous 'Promenade' uses just four of the original ten pieces from Mussorgsky's composition. ELP's *Pictures At An Exhibition* is structured as follows:

1. Promenade
2. The Gnome
3. Promenade
4. The Sage
5. The Old Castle
6. Blues Variations
7. Promenade
8. The Hut Of Baba Yaga
9. The Curse Of Baba Yaga
10. The Hut Of Baba Yaga
11. The Great Gates Of Kiev

With regards to the fact that ELP added a lot of their own ideas to their version of *Pictures At An Exhibition*, Emerson was quoted in *Beetle* in February 1974; "Even though they were written by us, they were inspired by Mussorgsky's original piece. 'Blues Variations' is really one of the phases of one of the movements in

How Does ELP's Version Compare To Mussorgsky's?

Pictures called the 'The Old Castle'. The actual thing goes very slow and mournful, so I just made it into a shuffle so there was a blues variation on that particular thing. Then Greg had the idea of the minstrel singing underneath the castle, which was 'The Sage'. So it all related to that. We had to sort of put our own thing into that as well. We put some of our own *Pictures At An Exhibition* into Mussorgsky's *Pictures At An Exhibition*".

Even within the framework of an existing composition, ELP always had the propensity to make it their own. Emerson was quoted in *Crawdaddy* in August 1971; "I know that now what I am in life is a musician and I shall always be one — that's what I know for a fact — and my output is as a performer and writing new things is an outlet for me and as long as I have those two outputs I shall be perfectly happy. Every time that I write something different, I try and make it different from the last thing which I wrote. At the moment, I can't say what the next thing that will come out of me, what it will be."

In the 2016 released deluxe edition, Chris Welch advocated of the piece in the liner notes; "There can be no grander opening statement in all music than 'Promenade' from *Pictures At An Exhibition*. While long the domain of symphony orchestras, it was the rock trio Emerson, Lake and Palmer that embraced the Russian composer Mussorgsky's magnificent work with astounding results when they performed concert versions of his suite."

Emerson plays organ on the opening 'Promenade'. It contains bars of 5/4 and 6/4 (some scholars advocated that Mussorgsky wanted to portray the uneven nature of the limp he had as he walked round the exhibition). The unusual use of time signatures in Mussorgsky's piece lends itself well to prog rock in such regard. Ironically perhaps, the title track on ELP's *Tarkus* album is also in 5/4. It is for different reasons but like Mussorgsky (perhaps!), ELP made a very deliberate decision to use 5/4 to portray meaning in their 'Tarkus' track.

Lake was quoted of *Tarkus* in *Melody Maker* in February 1971; "It's about the futility of conflict, expressed in this context in terms of soldiers at war — but it's broader than that. The words

ELP - *Pictures At An Exhibition*: In-depth

are about revolution, the revolution that's gone, that has happened. Where has it got anybody? Nowhere. It starts off with frustration, with the 5/4 piece, which in itself is a frustrating metre. The natural beat is four, so the extra beat every time is unnatural. Then it builds up towards the first song which asks the question: Why can't you see how stupid it is, conflict? The next song is about the hypocrisy of it all and the last song is the aftermath, the conclusion of it. What have we gained? The very last bit, the march, is a joke. It was written in six days and rehearsed in six. It all came very quickly from one idea. Keith started the instrumental piece, the 5/4, and I had my song at the very end. We figured it out on a piece of paper."

In both *Tarkus* and *Pictures At An Exhibition*, there is a strong sense that the 5/4 time signature wasn't used for its own sake. Greg Lake asserted; "Since the advent of progressive music, there had been a tendency among certain musicians to try and impress the public by performing songs in odd time signatures. These pieces usually sounded gratuitous and self indulgent to me, and I always thought that they were not as clever as they pretended to be. Often a piece claiming to be written in 5/4 was just 4/4 with an added beat pasted at the end of each bar. A proper 5/4, by contrast, would be 'Take Five' by Dave Brubeck or 'Mars, The Bringer Of War' by Holst. Those pieces were conceived using five beats to the bar from the start."

Emerson was quoted of *Tarkus* in *Prog* in 2011; "Why be governed and dictated to by a 4/4 or 3/4 rhythm by adding and subtracting notes just to make it fit?" Elsewhere he said, "When we recorded *Pictures* at Newcastle City Hall I played 'Promenade' on their huge pipe organ. We had a mobile unit outside and they recorded the whole concert. The tapes went back to Advision where Eddie Offord was the engineer. After I played 'Promenade' it was quite a long way to get down the steps from the organ, so Carl had to play a long drum roll as I came back on stage."

As with Mussorgsky's version, ELP then go into 'The Gnome' and they generally stay true to the original. It is particularly in Palmer's heavy drum solo and Emerson's synthesiser towards

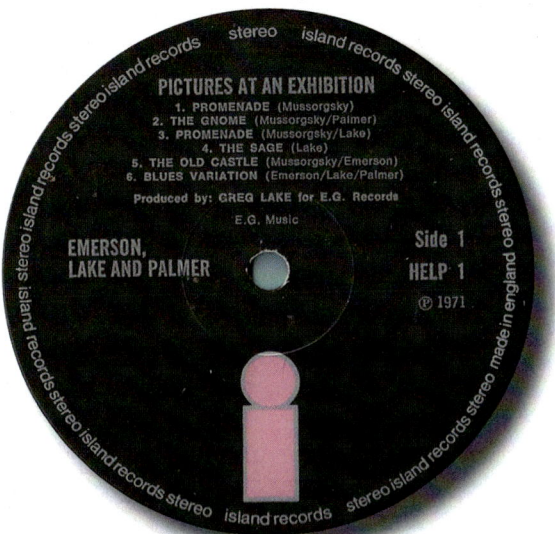

As with the previous two albums, *Pictures At An Exhibition* originally appeared in the UK on Chris Blackwell's Island label. The same label that Greg had been on with King Crimson.

In the States it was originally released on Cotillion, a subsidiary label of Atlantic.

A simple but effective design, depicting empty frames on the outer cover and images on the inside of the gatefold that represent the individual sections of the piece.

Although vinyl was the favoured format for most people in the early seventies, in the States both 8-track cartridge and open reel tapes were also popular.

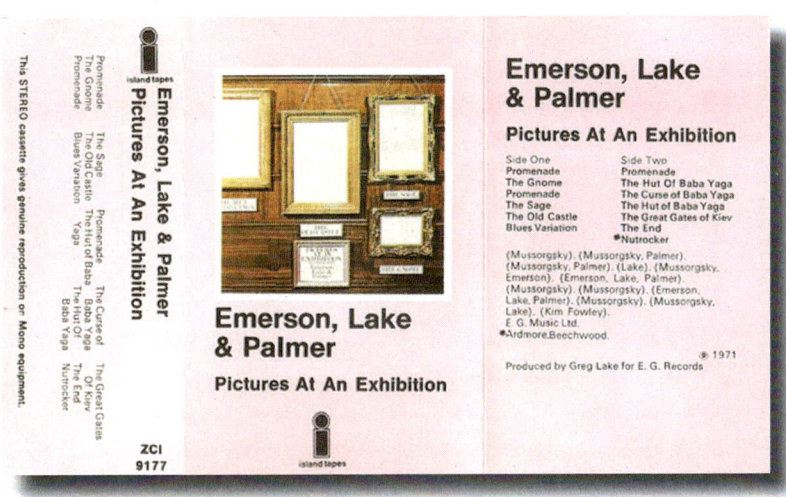

The cassette format proved popular in the UK. Top: An original Island release, and below it, a reissue on the band's own label Manticore that was formed in 1973 following the success the band had achieved in the previous three years.

The album was released on various different labels around the world. In several countries it was released on Atlantic, including Japan and Australia. The version here is another Atlantic release, from Venezuela.

In Brazil it was released on Atco, an Atlantic subsidiary label.

As with the UK, other European countries originally released the album on Island although as these variations from the Netherlands and France show, Island's newly designed "palm tree" label was used, as opposed to the black version used in the UK.

There wasn't much in the way of design variations on the cover but in Japan the album was released with the ubiquitous obi strip. In some countries the album was released in a single sleeve so the images on the inside were used on the other cover as in this variation from Brazil.

How Does ELP's Version Compare To Mussorgsky's?

the end of this section that really makes it unique to ELP. "'The Gnome' turned out to be quite a bit of fun, particularly between me and Carl," recalled Emerson. "It took a lot of us looking at each other to play the answering phrases between the organ and drums. Sometimes I'd fool with him and wait a split second before playing the next bit."

Back into the second 'Promenade' and Lake's lyrics set to the original melody add something new to the piece. The meaning behind the lyrics has largely been considered as grossly ambiguous among ELP fans over the years but really, there were multiple instances in which Lake advocated in favour of using such an abstract approach to his writing.

He was quoted in *Circus* in August 1977; "My lyrics are mostly influenced by life experiences — not books or anything — just wisdoms you grow up learning to be true. I'm particularly interested in things that are universally true. It's actually just a stage I'm going through. I mean, I can actually see myself going through it. I know I'll come through it with less concern for the truth, but right now it's very important to me. I still feel I haven't exhausted the possibilities of writing within this framework. I can't think of any songwriter who's exploited the subject as much as I have. But I come from that sort of heritage. I was in a group called King Crimson before ELP and that was a 'thinking band'. I mean, you have to make up your mind early on — you're either going to go for a quick commercial kill or you decide at some point that you're going to be a real artist, and I made that decision back then. It's something all painters go through. You go through a stage where you have to feel satisfied with yourself technically before you can relax and do things that are just emotive. I'm more of a romantic than anyone else in the band. In terms of music, I believe in beautiful things rather than bizarre things. I'd rather have harmony than dissonance. I know there's lots of dissonance in this band but it's that contrast that makes music dynamic. If you have either element on their own, it's just not as dynamic."

'The Sage' was composed entirely by Greg Lake but it is still in line with the theme of Mussorgsky's piece in that Lake's writing was inspired by the idea of a minstrel singing underneath a castle (i.e. Mussorgsky's 'The Old Castle'). In response to a reader's question in *Melody Maker* in October 1973, Greg wrote; "As a rule most of what I write is the result of imagination and not based on actual experiences." The sentimental mood of this section is pretty much characteristic of one of Lake's philosophies on music. He recalled in his autobiography; "I have always seen music as something magical. As a young boy of five or six years old, I heard the medieval tune of 'Greensleeves' playing on the radio. I was emotionally touched by its magical power. I had heard lots of music before, of course — Vera Lynne and all that sort of stuff, which was popular at the time — but that piece taught me that music could really mean something, and that it could touch people personally... There is a feeling of suspension and then relief, which draws you in and makes you react emotionally."

ELP have 'The Old Castle' as their fifth movement and musically, it only relates to Mussorgsky's movement of the same title to a very loose extent. This is largely due to the fact that Emerson strongly showcases the capabilities of the Moog at this point. That said, Emerson's synthesiser solo incorporates rhythms that Mussorgsky used in his composition of 'The Old Castle'.

Emerson was quoted in *Circus* in March 1972; "I use the Moog more harmonically, not really as a sound source. I do sort of extend the possibilities of the Moog to noise which is not musical, but not as much as I mainly use it as a harmonic instrument. I'd reached the stage on the organ where I was getting sounds out of it which even the Hammond Organ Company hadn't built the instrument for. Using the Moog synthesiser I had all these sounds more readily at my fingertips and a lot of other sounds as well." Upon being asked whether he liked to use a synthesiser to replicate sounds such as trumpet and violin, he was quoted in the same feature; "I've gone to great lengths to imitate these sounds. But mainly I use it to create new ones."

In response to a reader's question in *Melody Maker* in September 1972, Lake wrote; "My guitars are a Gibson J200 with Guild strings, which I played on 'The Old Castle'." Emerson;

How Does ELP's Version Compare To Mussorgsky's?

"I've always liked a good shuffle and we turned 'The Old Castle' into a blues that became 'Blues Variation'. We also played another version of 'Promenade', this time with the band." 'Blues Variations' is a sped up version of Mussorgsky's main theme from 'The Old Castle' played over a twelve bar blues based structure.

Following this, more variations are played before a version of 'Promenade' loyal to Mussorgsky's links into ELP's eighth movement; 'In The Hut Of Baba Yaga' and then 'The Curse Of Baba Yaga', both of which are based on sections from Mussorgsky's 'The Hut On Fowls' Legs'. It is during 'The Curse Of Baba Yaga' that ELP have (what sounds like!) a moment of improvisation. That said though, there are parts that sound a little reminiscent of 'The Gnome'. ELP's 'The Hut Of Baba Yaga' is predominantly faithful to Mussorgsky's original. With the exception of Lake's lyrics and Emerson's frenzied exploitation of the organ, 'The Great Gates Of Kiev' is also largely faithful to Mussorgsky's version.

With the performance only lasting around thirty-three minutes the album included an additional track. "We did B. Bumble and the Stinger's 'Nut Rocker' as an encore, because the audience were demanding we came back on stage," recalled Emerson. To which Lake was quoted; "Yes, we did 'Nut Rocker' at the end. I love the music history and the part of it that goes back to the wonderful fifties rock 'n' roll era."

As paradoxical as it probably sounds, Emerson's approach to improvisation was very structured in terms of how he was clear about where and when he felt it would work, and indeed wouldn't. He was quoted in *Crawdaddy* in August 1971; "Some pieces don't require an improvisation at all and some pieces do. Some pieces don't contain any improvisation. A number like 'Rondo' requires a lot of improvisation and a number like 'Take A Pebble' is one where you feel it's right to improvise."

In the case of *Pictures At An Exhibition*, the sections that are loyal to Mussorgsky's original composition contrast with where ELP added their own take on things. Which bits of ELP's compositions were planned and which were structured? Well,

ELP - *Pictures At An Exhibition*: In-depth

there's not necessarily any way of being certain on that one. Such was the fluency of their musicianship.

It is interesting to consider how ELP's version of *Pictures At An Exhibition* may have taken shape — from how it was played in earlier performances right up to what it was by the time it came to be recorded at Newcastle City Hall in March 1971. It was reported in *Melody Maker* in October 1970; "Emerson, Lake and Palmer must be the brightest hopes for many a long year. Reputation alone won them their award in the *Melody Maker* poll and now they are proving themselves. At Watford last Thursday they had a capacity crowd stamping and cheering as they pounded through material old and new with the ruthless competence and exaggerated showmanship that Keith Emerson inspires. Comparisons with The Nice are inevitable but here is a trio that takes off where The Nice stopped. With only three appearances behind them before the Watford gig, they could be forgiven for taking a while to warm up, but once they did there was no stopping them. Keith Emerson and Moog is a combination that had to happen. Having squeezed every possible sound from his Hammonds, the Moog was the natural progression — and the £4000 computer-like gadget that sits amid the speakers brings out a variety of space fiction noises once reserved for the studio only. Greg Lake and Carl Palmer assure you it's not a mark two version of The Nice. Greg uses acoustic guitar on several numbers, playing almost classical style, and takes the vocal seat, while Carl's drumming holds the whole thing together. Speed is his greatest asset as he proved in his solo during 'Rondo'. 'Rondo' is the only Nice number ELP feature and the arrangement has been changed to suit the new trio. But it still brings out the most in Keith, dressed in glittery tail suit, who leaps on to his organ and chucks his knife into the speaker cabinet. *Pictures At An Exhibition* — Keith's major new opus — showed us what the Moog is capable of, though Keith admits he is still learning how to use it. Dramatic vocals, a wah-wah bass solo, some slick replying between bass and drums and organ and tasteful acoustic guitar work make up this twenty-minute piece, which brought the fans to their feet. 'Take A Pebble', Greg Lake's

How Does ELP's Version Compare To Mussorgsky's?

composition, features Keith plucking the piano strings inside the lid and perfect brush work from Carl, and 'Knife-Edge' shows the band at its heaviest. For an encore they gave us a rockin' version of the old B. Bumble number, 'Nut Rocker', which had the idiot dancers bopping in the aisles. An ideal climax to a show which proved that ELP are worthy of their brightest hope award."

With it being reported that *Pictures At An Exhibition* was only twenty minutes long as part of one of ELP's earlier live performances, it raises a question as to what earlier versions of ELP's piece sounded like; had they begun to add their own sections or was their version mostly reliant on just material from Mussorgsky's original piece at this stage? Did Emerson use the Moog in slightly different ways compared to the rendition of the piece that was recorded in Newcastle City Hall on 26th March 1971? It is a possibility based on how ELP was still in the very early days as a band and in terms of how experimenting with the possibilities of the Moog was seemingly a constant feature throughout Emerson's use of it in his career.

Certainly, the Moog was an important aspect of ELP's sound from the early days of the band's tenure. It was reported in *Beat Instrumental* in January 1971; "One of the more remarkable aspects of ELP's music is their creative use of that Frankenstein of the group world — the Moog synthesiser. Emerson has his model set up on a chrome stand just behind his A100 (where he can get at it) and he probably displays more feel for the capabilities of this extraordinary machine than any other contemporary musician. Bob Moog built a special programmer console for Keith — which is mounted on top of the synthesiser proper — and it is this quick-change device that enables Emerson to make the most of the Moog. There are millions of sound combinations available from synthesisers and the use of a pre-set device (with programmed cards, rather like a computer) greatly minimises the need for time consuming adjustments. On the *Emerson, Lake and Palmer* album, 'Tank' is the best choice for a Moog showcase. A brisk Palmer solo leads — via some effective phasing — to Moogsville. Monstrous backup tracks mount in crescendos, and then Emerson enters the ribbon-control on top of it all, creating wild and heathen sounds that stun the eardrums."

Chapter Four

A Continuing Legacy

From the beginning of their tenure, it comes across that ELP had a long-term plan and were creatively and commercially ambitious. Lake was quoted in *Disc & Music Echo* in July 1971; "The first aim of a band is to become successful. Next year, for our own gratification, we'll probably turn to more inventive things. Hopefully, you use a successful position to create new things and open new fields for other people. I think that for us there are a lot of alternatives."

ELP had performed *Pictures At An Exhibition* live many times before releasing one performance of it as an album. Despite the delay in getting it released, eventually, it was given a chance. Emerson was quoted in *Circus* in March 1972; "We're very concerned with doing new things. Every time we do an album, if it sounds like something we've done on the other albums we reject it. We're into progressing and music to us is a challenge, but we don't put the end result on a record until the public has heard it. When we work with an audience live, we can tell how they're reacting to a piece."

Owing to the fact that *Pictures At An Exhibition* was recorded live and was subject to all of the limitations of such, the piece really is an achievement. Palmer was quoted in *Hit Parader* in January 1972; "There are problems in creating our arrangements on stage. As far as the complexity of our music is concerned, it would be very easy for us to advance this on stage, but naturally we couldn't get the effects arrived at from overdubbing in the studio."

It was never plain sailing for ELP in terms of reviews. *Pictures*

ELP - *Pictures At An Exhibition*: In-depth

At An Exhibition was reviewed in the *Coventry Evening Telegraph* in January 1972; "Favourites on the college circuit but yet to break into the commercial market beyond. Before this record, their music was tasty enough for wider consumption. Now it has seemed to move totally to the region of specialised, minority appeal. There are some interesting rhythms exposed to expert musicianship and certain sound innovations that don't seriously disturb the flow of the music. But in general, the group appear far more concerned with effect than with entertainment — perhaps because it is a live recording. In a studio they might still be impressive."

Some questions that I would love to be able to ask the reviewer are as follows: "Don't you like it when a band tries to put something a little different out there?" "What was it about the album that you didn't find entertaining?" They are not questions that I would want to ask in a derogatory or accusatory way — there is no accounting for taste and all opinions are valid because music is so subjective. It's just really fascinating how in terms of the album and really, how the band are perceived overall, their work often seemed to (and still continues to) divide opinion so much. Oh well, one person's music is another person's noise and really, something really important about the legacy of ELP and their music is the fact that whilst they were perhaps seen as an acquired taste — artistically and commercially — they still made a tremendous impact. Emerson was quoted in *Keyboard* in November 2010; "Well, *Pictures At An Exhibition* was recorded live, with no editing or overdubbing. What you hear is exactly what happened on that particular night."

It is impossible to comment on any of the band's performances of *Pictures At An Exhibition* that weren't recorded. The demands of the piece, both technically and in terms of its length, are such that there may have been some gigs where ELP delivered something that was lacking. I doubt that it would have been to a tremendous extent based on their level of technical ability as musicians, but still, human error and all that. Either way, to even attempt to play an extended version of an established classical piece is a brave choice for a three-piece band and, based on the recording from

A Continuing Legacy

Newcastle City Hall alone, it was arguably a good idea.

Not long after the recording of, ELP were on a roll with their live performances. It was reported in *Sounds* in April 1971; "ELP always have something new to offer on their gigs and Wednesday night at Leicester's De Montfort Hall was no exception. Not only did they play many of the established favourites but included two samples from the new album due out in May. 'Tarkus' — the title track taking up one side of the album — is a half-hour affair which shows all three musicians at their best. Starting in 5/4 time the number progresses through innumerable time changes bringing it all up to the pitch of hysteria. There are some beautiful organ passages included, with the heated drumming of Carl powering the number on, and featuring poignant vocals of Greg, to the setting of his thoughtful and exact lead work. The second sampler — 'Jeremy Bender' — was a quick country tune with a jolly beat and a constant melody. And judging from the reception the numbers were given, the album is going to be a seller. In spite of a subdued start to the evening ELP received standing ovations to most of the numbers from the 2,500 who filled the hall. *Pictures At An Exhibition* — with Keith playing the organ — opened the second set and they followed with 'Take A Pebble'. Keith now incorporates a lot more showmanship and comedy into the act — springing into the audience and creating some way-out sound effects. By the time the synthesised hissing of steam and chugging engines filled the hall everybody was on their chairs ready for the inevitable 'Rondo'. The way Keith spans the organ, hurls it across the stage, and lies under it squeezing our grunts of electronic pain makes me think he is trying to kill the last bit of The Nice left in him — which the music certainly does. The only possible encore was 'Nut Rocker' which brought the fans to the front of the stage, rocking with the band as they finished a night which bettered the gig there last year."

It was reported in *Melody Maker* in April 1971; "Emerson, Lake and Palmer performed the first pop concert in Wigan, a town generally deprived of progressive music, for over three years at the town's ABC cinema. The trio blew into the mill town like a

ELP - *Pictures At An Exhibition*: In-depth

TNT explosion last Thursday and played to an ecstatic audience of 2,000 and a handful of police officers. The tremendous reputation that has grown up around these three young musicians in such a short time was more than justified as Emerson and Co. displayed dexterity and total mastery over their instruments. They played jazz, rhythm and blues, classical and folk music with such subtle transitions that any anomalies between the styles went unnoticed before even the most competent progressive musician. The group revolved around Keith Emerson. As a showman he was terrific — dragging several hundredweights of Hammond organ across the stage that has regrettably become almost an anachronism in Wigan. Jumping over it and pulling it down onto the stage floor with him, Keith was playing two organs simultaneously for much of the night. He played the grand piano as if it were a guitar, coming down into the audience with a wailing portmanteau and disappearing into the Gents with it. Greg Lake and Carl Palmer were not without their moments. Lake's haunting, poignant voice and guitar solos came as peaceful contrasts to the World War Three sounds that thundered across the auditorium when the group was in full swing. Carl Palmer as the percussionist had the difficult job of keeping time for an ensemble that seems to play at twice the speed of the average group. An immaculate solo in the finale brought a fitting climax to his performance and three girls in the upstairs auditorium standing on their seats to display identical red hot pants with the words 'Carl The Greatest'. The group played numbers from their first album, the title track of their forthcoming album, *Tarkus*, and as an item of nostalgia for fans of the now defunct Nice group, 'Rondo'."

Lake recalled; "The last show on this leg of the UK tour was played in Wigan on 1st April 1971. Not so many well-known bands came to play in Wigan so none of us really knew what to expect. As is often the case in smaller towns and cities though, the audience was fantastic. It was one of those special nights when everything just seemed to go right and the atmosphere in the room was truly electrifying. People often ask me to name my favourite ELP performance and, of course, the ones that often spring to mind

A Continuing Legacy

are the big festivals and the more historic events. Looking back now however, I think that some of ELP's greatest performances took place in the small city halls in the United Kingdom and the United States during the early days of the band's career."

Pictures At An Exhibition is a vital ingredient of ELP's legacy. It became an important part of their identity and it continued to be a strong point of reference long after its release. It was reported in *Gig* in September 1977; "Back on the road for the first time in almost three years, ELP have returned with a refreshing degree of levity and good humour, contrasting sharply with the austere behaviour they've come to be known for. After the instrumental 'The Enemy God Dances With The Black Spirits', Emerson introduces *Pictures At An Exhibition* as 'another number you can all sing along to'."

When prefacing an interview with Greg Lake, *The Daily Mirror* advocated in October 1972; "You have never seen Greg Lake on *Top Of The Pops* or heard him on Radio One, and yet his rock group — Emerson, Lake and Palmer — are in the superstar class. The more high-brow music papers have been raving about the group since their formation in 1969 (sic) and they've just walked off with seven top awards. But you don't hear them on air because they've never released a single. Singles may get the most airtime but albums make the most money, and all their four releases are million-dollar sellers. Greg is singer, musician, writer and producer of the exciting group which has turned today's serious rock fans onto the classics. Their electronic version of the Russian composer Mussorgsky's *Pictures At An Exhibition* is a highlight of their stage act."

From the tentative days of being heavily criticised by John Peel, ELP had come a long way. It was considered in *Crawdaddy* in August 1971; "Keith Emerson was back at the Isle of Wight, this time with Lake and Palmer, last summer. The 1970 Festival gave us their debut — and gave Emerson the kind of recognition, and the kind of atmosphere that time around, that he'd long deserved. And then once again, things built up from there. They got voted 'Brightest Hope' by the readers of Britain's best overground

ELP - *Pictures At An Exhibition*: In-depth

music paper, the *Melody Maker*. Their first album sold very fast in England, and by January they had another in the can (which is being released this month over here). The only sour note came after the band's first London gig, when John Peel, top 'progressive' DJ, called the show 'A tragic waste of talent and electricity'. Not many people agreed with Peel, however, and before their current US gigs, ELP squeezed in a twenty-six-night British tour. And what a tour! For Keith Emerson it was a triumphal return to the circuits. When I saw the show, at Plymouth, Emerson said how good it felt 'to be back where we started from' — and his sincerity was obvious. Obvious too was his supremely confident flexibility, as he handled all the equipment he had on stage: two electric organs, Bechstein Grand piano, electric clavinet, plus $12,000-worth of Moog synthesiser. For two and a half hours they played, giving us highlights from the first album and astonishingly tight, precision-work previews of the second — including the marathon title-piece 'Tarkus' and a stunning re-working of Mussorgsky's *Pictures At An Exhibition* (which they've been leaving out on their American gigs). They brought in a beautiful series of solos. Carl Palmer's drumming had flair, abrasion and always the right texture. Greg Lake's guitar-work was a real delight. He handled himself with a kind of unassuming majesty, making the switches seem easy from electric to bass and then to an acoustic that he gracefully coaxed into sounding like a harpsichord at times. And Keith Emerson. He wasn't playing superstar, he was part of the group. He even avoided all those old Nice numbers that everyone wanted to hear (until the encore, when 'Rondo' suddenly re-emerged, better than ever, with that old train-whistle blowing the roof off the theatre). Yet despite what was almost self-effacement, Emerson's performance — especially, I thought, on piano — was a real tour-de-force. What a musician. The audience response was tremendous. There had been mass excitement and a kind of jubilant anticipation beforehand; and then, with the performance, the response grew to an all-smiles, dancing-in-the-aisles ovation. The group's reception was the same on all twenty-five nights. Each date wound up with the audience dancing to the late great 'Nut Rocker' done on electric

A Continuing Legacy

clavinet. In America — by way of a strange kind of contrast — the group has had to drop this number because people haven't seemed familiar with it. And they've found this surprising, because in England 'Nut Rocker' is regarded as a classic oldie and copies of the original single — by a bunch of American session men who called themselves B. Bumble and the Stingers — are very much treasured. Along with Kokomo's 'Asia Minor' it was one of the first rock sorties into classical music. A real beginning, in fact, for Emerson, Lake and Palmer."

ELP clearly put thought into how their work needed to be adapted to suit different audiences. Emerson was quoted in *Circus* in March 1972; "They generally stay quiet 'til the end in England, whereas American audiences react in the middle of something, which is rather exciting and inspires you."

He was quoted in *Crawdaddy* in August 1971; "I think that we're more advanced in England — maybe not advanced but we're willing to try. There's lots of room in England for people who want to do new things. Before I joined this band I'd never played a piano on stage in concert like we have done. Over here, I've never seen an American band do it, they always have an electric piano."

In July 1972, *New Musical Express* reported on a performance that ELP did in Switzerland; "'Fingers' is, of course, the focal point of the action on stage and there he is on his back with the organ on top of him and musically raping the contraption. He thrashes the keyboard, rocks and rides it across the stage and finally hurls it about, raising great clouds of blanco to smother the hordes of photographers and all the time the most amazing sounds are happening. He has the damn thing in pain. Lesser musicians than Carl Palmer and Greg Lake might be swamped by his amazing virtuosity, but they are not. They follow him at every twist and turn of his switching styles, and off hand I cannot think of another percussionist in any contemporary group who could match him as Palmer does and even come out on top. Greg does much to provide the perfect balance between them and still gets his justifiable acclaim during solos with 'Lucky Man' and 'Take A Pebble'.

ELP - *Pictures At An Exhibition*: In-depth

All three together provide a unique identity which far transcends any individual. I cannot think of another group who get so many different styles into their act or indeed of musicians capable of adapting to them. During one piece of incredible dexterity, Emerson turned to honkytonk piano, blues, jazz, classic, boogie woogie and even threw in a touch of the *1812 Overture*. All my favourite items were there from *Tarkus*, *Pictures At An Exhibition* plus two new items from their new album, *Trilogy*: 'The Endless Enigma' and 'Hoedown'. Then, of course, the finale to end all finales 'Rondo' — which is a national anthem — although ELP are currently providing a recorded classical piece called *Church Windows* to send the customers home in a more tranquil mood. Despite this, I might add, this particular audience refused to go for almost fifteen minutes, during which they set up a non-stop roar of approval for music received and understood. They cheered when Greg switched to acoustic. They cheered when Carl used a gong. They cheered when Keith switched from piano to organ. They might very well have cheered if he had blown his nose."

In November 1972, the *Birmingham Daily Post* reported on ELP's performance at Birmingham's Odeon; "Emerson, Lake and Palmer gave an enthusiastic and exhilarating performance, demonstrating why so many people are talking favourably about their individual style. The energy they put into a hard night's work said much for their stamina and the regard they have for the packed houses that greet them wherever they play. Keith Emerson, with his various keyboard instruments, and Birmingham-born Carl Palmer on drums, particularly showed why one-night stands can be so gruelling for a travelling band. Emerson even ventured into the audience in the early stages, trailing with him part of the Moog synthesiser. Their music is the type that no one can like all the time and the softer numbers came as a welcome analgesic to some of the ear-shattering sounds with which they are more associated. Much of their music is reminiscent of the sadly defunct Nice band. Greg Lake's singing frequently suffered against the organ and drums in arrangements that seemed more like a battle than accompaniment. Highlights of the evening were the gentle songs.

A Continuing Legacy

'Take A Pebble' and 'Lucky Man' in which Lake's singing had a chance to show its true colours and *Pictures At An Exhibition*. Predictably, they played 'Nut Rocker' for an encore with Palmer's drum, gong and bell solo bringing strenuous response from the audience. An exciting night at the Odeon."

Material from the debut album and *Tarkus* are also important in the band's overall legacy. Tracks (and indeed imagery in the form of the *Tarkus* armadillo) were relevant to live sets for years to come. ELP's performance at London's Oval cricket ground was reviewed in *Circus* in January 1973; "As the crowd roared their approval, the group raced from backstage, launching immediately into 'Hoedown', the upbeat, good-humoured number from their recent *Trilogy* LP, and the crowd was on its feet. Without hesitation, the group jumped immediately into 'Tarkus', and simultaneously pulled off the biggest feat in the history of rock wizardry. Two mammoth armadillo tanks appeared on both sides of the stage, bellowing replicas of the figures on the *Tarkus* cover. The metal dragons breathed clouds of smoke, and, as the show thundered to its climactic high point, the tanks thundered an ear-deafening barrage, driving fans into a wild frenzy of excitement and jubilation. Keith pounded the piano as 'Take A Pebble' echoed from the massive multi-toned speakers, and Greg Lake brought down the house with his excellent acoustic guitar work on 'Lucky Man'. But with the advent of *Pictures At An Exhibition*, off the LP of the same name, the crowd watched in absolute amazement as Carl Palmer's drum solo threatened to pop the sliver of sun out of the darkening sky. In a fury, Carl hurled himself at the drum kit, battering the cymbals and destroying the gongs. The *Tarkus* tanks belched forth their deafening roar as London's last great rock concert of the season shrieked to its end — and ELP proved once again that they remain the world's greatest rock band, upholding their title of Britain's Best Band, (the title they won last year) and taking on the title of World's Best Band as well. As the last fans wearily straggled home, ELP slowly unwound backstage, gathering the remains of their shattered instruments with them. Each clutched at their golden trophies: Top Group, British and

ELP - *Pictures At An Exhibition*: In-depth

International; Emerson's tribute as the top keyboard man; Palmer's trophy as top drummer; Lake's souvenir as the world's most accomplished producer; ELP as the top pop arrangers; and finally the shared award, Keith Emerson and Greg Lake taking honours as the world's top composers."

It was reported in the *Acton Gazette* in December 1972; "Emerson, Lake and Palmer have never had a hit single and you have never seen them on *Top Of The Pops* but it was like a full-scale invasion when their fans swarmed to see them at Hammersmith Odeon on Saturday. Successful as the other recent concerts have been at this ever-improving music venue, they never even approached the popularity of ELP. This fast-growing cult group have gained their following not by elaborate stage acts, flashy clothes or expensive publicity stunts, but simply by being three very talented musicians. It is very difficult to be indifferent about Emerson, Lake and Palmer — you either like them or you loathe them. It certainly did not take long to discover how the wall-to-wall audience at the Odeon felt about them. They stamped, shouted, whistled and clapped both in recognition at the start of each number, and in appreciation at the end of it. The stage itself looked set for a scene out of some bizarre science fiction play, with banks of speakers and amplifiers, flashing lights and all the twinkling electronic paraphernalia that surrounds organist extraordinaire Keith Emerson. There were even a couple of giant model monsters, which breathed fire and smoke at various points during the proceedings. To their fans, their unique brand of futuristic music is as far removed from the ordinary 'pop' scene as it is from Beethoven or Bach. Drawing a lot of its influence from jazz, it has the same indescribable compulsion for those who like and a complete incomprehension for those who do not. The star of the evening, if there was one, was undoubtedly Keith Emerson, who flitted between organ, Moog, piano and back to organ again, like some demonic electrician, throwing switches and pushing in plugs to produce the most incredible sounds. At the same time, the drummer Carl Palmer hammered away as if his life depended on it, using a few extra percussive nick-nacks such as two enormous

A Continuing Legacy

Chinese gongs, cylindrical chimes and even a Moog drum. It may not really be music in the purest sense, but as entertainment, you only had to hear the deafening shouts for more at the close of the show if you wanted proof of its effect on the audience."

It was reported in the *Harrow Observer* in October 1972; "Fantastic. An incredible musical spectacle. Undoubtedly the most talented group of the decade — that, in my opinion, is the only way to describe Emerson, Lake and Palmer. And if you think I'm exaggerating, ask the 20,000 pop fans who crowded into the Oval for the *Melody Maker* Poll Awards concert on Saturday, and I am sure they will agree. Keith Emerson is a brilliant pianist, organist and one of the few who can really play the synthesiser. Carl Palmer is a drummer who can play a set of twenty drums for two hours without missing a beat. Greg Lake is a brilliant guitarist who provides the vocals. However, vocally the group is nothing, and to be quite frank, Greg Lake has no depth to his voice, which is the only weak link in what is otherwise a musically perfect group. Their music is very much influenced by the classical composers. Some is tuneful, other numbers are based on a pulsating beat, which can send an audience into a hypnotic trance. They played for two hours on Saturday, during which time two giant model hedgehogs on either side of the stage puffed smoke from their nostrils. The end of the act was incredible. The stage was immersed in orange smoke, Carl Palmer used microphones for drum sticks and Keith Emerson managed to get his Moog synthesiser playing as if a complete orchestra was on stage."

I trust that by hedgehogs, the reviewer was referring to the *Tarkus* models! I can see how they might have been recognised as hedgehogs to be fair. Of Greg Lake's singing, it is difficult to comment because live performances are always demanding on a singer (it is rumoured that this is why Lake was chewing gum in ELP's iconic performance at the California Jam in 1974). What really stands out in the latter report is the fact that so much stamina and accuracy was apparent in ELP's live performance and this is certainly the case on *Pictures At An Exhibition*.

Lake was quoted in *New Musical Express* in July 1972;

ELP - *Pictures At An Exhibition*: In-depth

"Receptions have been great. In Italy they were just completely amazed and in Berlin I thought we'd started another bloody war. You can always tell when it is going to be a big one in Europe. They turn out the army, the riot squad and the police — it was a bit like that in Germany. It's only when you come out to places like this and begin to travel these distances you really appreciate how small the world really is and how little difference there is between nationalities. We mostly all want the same things and the only barrier is language which we can at least break down with music. You can't really analyse your own success, but I think one of the reasons we have been accepted so broadly is that we don't strike attitudes or attempt to indoctrinate people. Occasionally, we present an idea, but we don't brainwash people."

Even during the success of the *Brain Salad Surgery* days, *Pictures At An Exhibition* made a strong contribution to ELP's live set. It was reported in *Beetle* in February 1974; "An Emerson, Lake and Palmer concert could not let down any ELP fan. They perform in entirety, *Tarkus*, *Pictures At An Exhibition*, and 'Karn Evil 9'. Add to this, from the first album, *Emerson, Lake and Palmer*, 'Lucky Man', and 'Take A Pebble', from *Trilogy*, the show's opener, Aaron Copland's 'Hoedown' and the rest of *Brain Salad Surgery*, 'Jerusalem', 'Toccata', 'Still...You Turn Me On', and 'Benny The Bouncer'. They also performed the King Crimson song, 'Epitaph' much to everyone's amazement. There are only a handful of bands that play for two and a half hours, and of these none, that I know of, play tracks from everything they have ever released, including four extended works of the magnitude of 'Take A Pebble', *Tarkus*, *Pictures At An Exhibition*, and 'Karn Evil 9'."

With *Tarkus* having confirmed ELP's position commercially in 1971 and with *Pictures At An Exhibition* being seen as something of a side project, in 1972, *Trilogy* moved somewhat away from the use of classical music influences. With new material from the *Trilogy* album added into the set list, ELP began to use less content from *Pictures At An Exhibition*. Material from the latter went on to become the stuff of ELP encores in later years. *Trilogy* went gold in the US and the song 'From The Beginning' made ELP's music

A Continuing Legacy

accessible to a wider audience. Despite the album's achievements though, it wasn't the success that ELP's earlier albums were.

Trilogy was reviewed in the *Coventry Evening Telegraph* in July 1972; "The trio that sound like an orchestra once keyboard master Keith Emerson gets under way on Moog synthesiser, mini Moog, organ and piano. There is variety indeed throughout, with 'Abaddon's Bolero' based on the Ravel piece — a real tour de force. It follows the line of adaptations of classical pieces Emerson has pursued since the Nice. This LP is aptly titled and Greg Lake's vocals and Carl Palmer's percussion add to the attack."

It was reviewed in the *Buckinghamshire Examiner* in July 1972; "The combined musical talents of Emerson, Lake and Palmer are more than capable of producing work that is not only musically competent but original and inventive too. But somewhere along the line they have got tied up in themselves, and the music has become too stale. There is a little of the originality that Keith Emerson displayed with The Nice. Perhaps not surprisingly, the band has all but been taken over by Emerson, with his organ, piano and Moog synthesiser. But listening to his performance on the band's new album, *Trilogy*, it seemed it has all been heard before. In fact, on the first side, there is little of note except 'From The Beginning' — dominated by Greg Lake's acoustic guitar work. In fairness, the poor first side is balanced by a good second side, which includes the long title track 'Trilogy'. The only other tracks are 'Living Sin' and 'Abaddon's Bolero'. The band has been together for some time now — and *Trilogy* must be a turning point for them. They should either change their musical direction or split up, because they are offering nothing new to their followers."

Trilogy was reviewed in the *Reading Evening Post* in August 1972; "I received this record just before I left on holiday and in those two weeks (holidays are always too short) it has jumped into the album charts, so it is obviously already a hit with ELP fans. It is up to the usual high standard we have all come to expect from this trio, but I felt like it fell a little short of *Tarkus* and *Pictures At An Exhibition*. It doesn't have a strong theme like those two, and at times I felt it was more of an exercise in what sort of sounds Emerson could get out of his Hammond and Moog. But once I forced that 'treasonable' thought out of my mind, I quite enjoyed the album, particularly Greg Lake's smooth 'From The Beginning'."

The reviewer makes a good point about how *Pictures At An Exhibition* (and indeed *Tarkus*) benefitted from having a strong sense of theme. *Pictures At An Exhibition* — both ELP's version and Mussorgsky's original — has a lot going for it as a piece because it has a sense of setting, character and indeed recurring musical ideas. In such regard, you could perhaps even go as far as to say that Mussorgsky's original piece had many qualities that lent itself to having strong potential as material for a prog rock album.

Despite ELP's reluctance to release *Pictures At An Exhibition* and despite the fact that upon its release they were keen to advocate that they didn't really count it as an album, the fact that it has been used as a strong point of comparison in relation to their later albums is testament to the impact it had as an ELP landmark in its own right.

Even after the release of *Pictures At An Exhibition*, there were still instances in which ELP were keen to advocate that it was pretty much a side project. Upon being asked how a group with the composing abilities of ELP started off by adapting whole pieces of classical music, Emerson was quoted in *Circus* in March 1972; "When we started playing in England, *Pictures* was like a blueprint to get the group's musical direction together. Mainly just to get out a whole thing and play it together. We had to learn how to play together 'cause we hadn't really got a system of writing our own music. It takes a long time for musicians to understand each others' musical thinking and be able to sort of put them together. It's only since *Tarkus* that we really got into a good system of writing together, so *Pictures* was like a first stage. We played it all around England and people wanted it, so we decided to give it to them. Since we've been coming over to America we've gotten into a whole new thing like *Tarkus*, and we only played *Pictures* once at Carnegie Hall. We don't look on it as a third album, just a good vibe."

Emerson was quoted in *The New York Times* in December 1973; "Classical rock is certainly not the correct description. Adaptations of classical pieces, which we do because we genuinely like the music, are not really what this band is about. Most of the material in our concerts and on our records is our own. I can spend three or four months working on my own music and after this, it is kind of a break, a refreshing change, to play something like 'Hoedown,' which incidentally is a lot of fun, or *Pictures At An Exhibition*. I'm not denying that I'm affected by classical music and I sometimes arrange my original music in a classical form. I suppose if you're looking for a description of what ELP is about, it's progressive rock with a lot of regard for the past."

With two studio albums and *Pictures At An Exhibition* behind them, in an interview with *Circus* in March 1972, Emerson was quoted in a way that suggested he didn't count *Pictures At An Exhibition* as ELP's third album; "We've already recorded what we consider our third album, and it's totally different from *Tarkus*. There's no total concept on either side. There are individual pieces which have no connection with each other at all. There's a cowboy song, a hoedown type number, and there's a fugue which I wrote and another very grand piece of music. They all differ."

It was reported of *Trilogy* in *Circus* in September 1972; "There's a new ELP LP. They want it to be considered their third album, devaluing the *Pictures At An Exhibition* disc as a souvenir of a time when the whole concept of the trio was very new and shiny."

In a 1972 ELP tour programme, it was stated of *Pictures At An Exhibition*; "This was a budget album based on a classical piece. Originally intended as a free album to be included in with *Tarkus*."

Carl Palmer was quoted in *Record Collector* in February 2014; "We could sell it cheap because we recorded it live. The record company wanted to sell it at full price, so it went backwards and forwards and finally came out."

ELP - *Pictures At An Exhibition*: In-depth

It was considered in *Senior Scholastic* in October 1972; "With the exception of their live recording of Mussorgsky's *Pictures At An Exhibition*, an imagistic piece recounting the author's impressions of a particular art exhibit (which ELP adapted and changed to fit their particular conceptual framework) Emerson, Lake and Palmer don't really make literal use of classical music the way The Nice did. Classical themes continue to surface occasionally, as on their latest album with Aaron Copland's 'Hoedown', but Keith makes use of established melodies only because he finds it challenging to integrate them into an exciting and vital modern mode. A typical example is his version of the *Brandenburg Concerto* granted on to Dylan's 'Country Pie' which sounds like a bad joke until your hear the supremely successful result."

I advocate that it wasn't necessarily the case that Emerson was explicitly keen to reject classical music influences on the basis of choosing to write his own material. The two aren't mutually exclusive. Still though, *Pictures At An Exhibition* was arguably ELP's most explicit example of embracing classical music. Emerson was quoted in *Circus* in March 1972; "Pop music is simple rock and roll. We don't have a place in pop music, we have a place in music in general."

He was quoted in *Crawdaddy* in August 1971; "I listen to quite lot of things, I've got a wide taste. I like to put on a record of whatever happens to suit my mood. One minute I might like to listen to John Williams playing solo guitar, classical guitar or I might like to educate myself and want to put on a record which involves a lot of piano playing and get inspired that way. My record collection is pretty varied."

It was considered of ELP in *Beat Instrumental* in January 1971; "They have drawn heavily from nearly all the major musical influences of the past — and have added some of their own as well. At the moment they have been together for a matter of months. What will they sound like when those months have become years? Impossible (even for Emerson, Lake and Palmer) to say."

Palmer was quoted in *Crawdaddy* in August 1971; "Broadly

A Continuing Legacy

speaking, we're just a band of musicians because we cover so many different styles when we go on stage. We play like a country thing, we play what could only be called jazz, we play classical music, we cover the contemporary works, also the Baroque works of Bach — so you really couldn't say this band plays just rock 'n' roll... Our album sells very well. There must be a big majority of people who don't listen to rock 'n' roll. Like I don't think Hendrix is rock 'n' roll. One of the biggest beauties of the band is that you can't say that it's this way or that way — it's not just one thing, it's everything."

Whilst *Trilogy* may not have been as well received as previous albums, it is relative in the sense that it still made its mark both creatively and commercially and it was during this time that the ELP became more excessive in their live sets via the used of a portable stage and rotating drums.

This paved the way for their highly successful album, *Brain Salad Surgery* in 1973. *Brain Salad Surgery* was an ambitious album with the conceptual 'Karn Evil 9' dominating around three quarters of the LP. It was soon after that ELP embarked on a world tour in which the 1974 live album *Welcome Back My Friends To The Show That Never Ends* was recorded. It was advocated in *Beetle* in February 1974; "*Brain Salad Surgery* seems to be a return to the path that Emerson, Lake and Palmer embarked on with the first album and *Tarkus*. *Pictures At An Exhibition* and *Trilogy* seem to be unimportant side trips in relation to the development of Emerson, Lake and Palmer. The album is a thematic unit. The title, *Brain Salad Surgery*, sums up the whole of the album."

Brain Salad Surgery took nine months to complete. Lake was quoted in *New Musical Express* in November 1973; "It's certainly taken longer to write and put together than others, but after you've made four albums people expect a certain thing from you and it's harder to come up with something that'll surprise them. A lot of bands go into solo ventures to avoid the monotony of playing the same style of music. Although we'll get into solo albums ourselves one day, the real answer for us is just to work harder and longer within the band. So when we do make solo albums it won't be

ELP - *Pictures At An Exhibition*: In-depth

through frustration."

Emerson was quoted in *Circus* in March 1972; "Our sort of creativity comes in varying periods. We get long periods when there isn't any creativity, we go into a studio and nothing sounds right, you know. *Tarkus* was written in six days because there was an awful lot of inspiration and one idea triggered another idea, and it was a long series of ideas being triggered off of what we had already done... We didn't rush it. Before we went in we had ideas of what we would do. It was just a question of putting it in a good order."

He was quoted in *Keyboard* in November 2010; "I'm probably most fond of my *Piano Concerto* and *Tarkus*, because these pieces are now performed all over the world by some great orchestras and keyboardists. I'm very proud of the Tokyo Philharmonic's version of *Tarkus* because I never thought I'd see the day where an orchestra would actually play that stuff. It's like ninety people playing — it just blew me away."

Pictures At An Exhibition was certainly the outcome of a creatively inspired period in ELP's career. Emerson was quoted in *Beetle* in February 1974; "When the group started we went out on the road with our first album in the can and were almost through our second album. In fact, we stated doing *Pictures*. So, we were well ahead and we had always got something in the can. So consequently, it came bang-bang-bang-bang like that because we were one jump ahead. Sure enough, after a while we caught up with ourselves, not for a lack of inspiration — of course every band goes through a period of thinking, 'What do we do now?', not to change for the sake of being different but for the sake of pleasing yourself. Because of this there was a longer time between *Trilogy* and *Brain Salad Surgery*. I think most bands now manage to get out an album every year as it's become pretty well a standard thing. If you start rushing things out, then you are really cheating your audience. Every album that I bring out, to me is a milestone. It's got to stand the test of time."

Hard work was pretty much the order of the day for ELP throughout the early seventies. Lake was quoted in *New Musical*

A Continuing Legacy

Express in November 1973; "I don't believe in luck but I do feel lucky. I'm grateful that the days of thrashing up the motorway are over. I did six years of that so I feel I've paid my dues. Y'see I believe in input equals output. If the cats who're doing it today put enough into it — and that's an incredible amount — then they'll be heavy themselves one day. The reason why somebody like me likes luxury is that as a band we're incredibly busy, and if I get maybe one day off this month then I want to know I can live like a king. Many rock musicians come from a poor background and their main motive for putting any energy into rock music is to be a success in life — to prove themselves to their friends and their parents. Once they've done that they relax. As a band we've never felt like that, but have kept on working and creating simply for its own sake."

Such creativity was embedded in not just relying on a mechanical process. Lake was quoted of *Brain Salad Surgery* in the same feature; "For the first time we've cared less about exploiting the technical side of the band and looked very deeply into the harmonic and melodic structures. The only way I can put it is that it's got more soul, more feel. At least that's what we've gone for. I think it generates more energy than previous albums. Y'see that's not such an easy thing for us. Of course any good musician can play a funky beat, but we play a very special sort of music, and it's difficult to take our music from its very static arranged thing and play that same music with feeling."

Lake was quoted in *Circus* in January 1973; "I think the whole concert concept will become more showy to the point where it will almost become a gypsy caravan existence and that is what we're designing now. We'd like to carry on our own stage that we'd build into a concert hall; have our own PA and coach that we'd use as a dressing room. Every night, we'd go into the coach, which will be done out like a living room and it will be our home. We'll walk out onto our own stage, like home again. It will give an aura like a circus trip. And it will also give the artist a chance to come to the concert relaxed before he goes on."

It is understandable as to how the piano suspended and spinning in the air perhaps wasn't too farfetched of an idea when

ELP - *Pictures At An Exhibition*: In-depth

it came to doing a certain iconic performance in 1974.

Headlining the California Jam in 1974, ELP were at the peak of their popularity by the mid seventies. Disappointingly though, after reaching such heights, the group became less prolific towards the later half of the decade. Greg Lake had a hit in 1975 with 'I Believe In Father Christmas'. Keith Emerson released a single called 'Honky Tonk Train Blues' in 1976 and in March 1977, ELP released *Works Volume 1*. Each band member had their own side of the album with the fourth side being the collaborative one. *Works Volume II* followed in November 1977.

Works Volume 1 was reviewed in the *Hammersmith & Shepherds Bush Gazette* in April 1977 "Well here it is — the first record produce in a long, long time from the mighty ELP. And their ever-loving ever-patient legions of fans are certain to be more than delighted with the two-album set. Quite frankly, I've never been able to understand the overwhelming popularity of ELP. Apart from their lofty attitudes towards performing and recording, their music, while technically superb, has little to do with the excitement, feeling and spontaneity at the heart of our most major bands. This collection is a vehicle for excessive self indulgence by the three individual members, each taking a side to pursue his own projects and coming together only on side four. Keith Emerson's contribution takes the form of 'Piano Concerto Number One', highly classical and divided into three movements. It's okay if you like that sort of thing, but tedious otherwise. The most accessible section of the album comes from Greg Lake, his set a predictable bunch of gentle songs written by himself and Pete Sinfield. Carl Palmer, for his part, has thrown in a curious hotch-potch of ideas that sound somehow unfinished while side four, comprising of 'Fanfare For The Common Man' and 'Pirates' introduces for the first time the well-known distinctive sound of the band playing together. Personally, this is not an album I'd buy, but each one to his own — and there are going to be many thousands of people making this their own."

The reviewer's honesty is commendable; they have been honest about the fact that they have never really been that into

A Continuing Legacy

ELP so of course, that colours their assessment of ELP's 1977 album. On balance though, the reviewer went to great lengths to express the fact that as a group, ELP sounded very divided on the album, purely owing to the nature of how it had been structured with regards to track listings.

There is no getting past that point and it's an interesting one on the basis of how musically together the group appeared to be on *Pictures At An Exhibition*; the creative rapport on the recording made at Newcastle City Hall certainly sounds like it was there. But then again, there was never any denial of the fact that all three members of ELP were open to the possibility of doing solo albums, even back then.

It's understandable really on the basis that with so much talent in one band, it is inevitable that all three individuals would have had musical interests and niches that weren't compatible with each others'. Really though, even in the early days of the band, ELP consisted of three individuals who had strong ideas about what they wanted to do.

With regards to how he felt about his contribution on ELP's debut album, Lake was quoted in *Melody Maker* in February 1971; "I was very pleased actually. I had my song on the second side and on the group things I was a third of the music. I also produced the album, which was a lot of fun. I was pleased in so far as my personal output got laid down as I wanted it. I am not pleased with the album now, in that I don't think it is complete. As I explained earlier, it was down to individuals. But I shall be happy with the new one."

In the later half of the seventies, ELP hired an orchestra of seventy musicians to go on tour with them. Whilst it was an exciting and innovative idea, it wasn't an economic one and after just ten days the tour had to be scrapped. Clearly ELP were over ambitious with regards to the scope and limitations of how far they could take their classical music aspirations. Emerson was quoted in *Gig* in September 1977; "Musically it was like the bottom dropping out of my world when we had to drop the orchestra. I was very worried when we did the first gig without the orchestra because I thought the audience would feel cheated. In fact, they loved it. I was quite surprised because all the time I'd been thinking we've got to hit our audiences with something bigger and better. It came as a very encouraging shock when we discovered we really don't have to do all that; they'll love us anyway. That made me feel better."

Arguably, it goes back to the idea that, as was demonstrated in *Pictures At An Exhibition*, a three piece band can deliver on the classical front without an orchestra — especially via the use of the Moog. Emerson was quoted in *Beetle* in February 1974; "There's a lot more freedom with three people, less people to relate to. I can't see how another instrument could possibly fit in, there's just no room."

The factor of band dynamics is important too. Lake was quoted in *Disc* in October 1972; "It's much easier with three than four because so many things have got to fall into place for three, you wouldn't believe it when you add a fourth person. You don't add one more risk, you add fifty thousand more risks of it going wrong. You don't exactly consciously balance out personalities, you just try to give everyone else an easy time and you get an easy time back. I remember when I was in groups before I would really argue a lot — about petty things, maybe to do with the way a piece of music should go. But you learn to compromise and live together. I mean, we've learnt to live together twenty-four hours a day for the last three years. We very rarely have time off. We're working just about all the time."

Emerson was quoted in *Beetle* in February 1974; "Sound wise, the Moog can only stretch things. I used it for the first time with an orchestra; that was with The Nice and the London Philharmonic. That was one of the first ones that arrived in England and I had a guy sit down behind it, tuning the damn thing up as I was playing it. At the start of ELP I got a hold of Bob (Moog) and told him what I wanted to do. He made up a model, the first of its kind. I don't think they ever made any more. This one was made up, and I brought it back to England and worked on it. There were lots of teething problems to start with but there were great possibilities.

A Continuing Legacy

It enabled me to expand my musical ideas and make far more things possible to do musically, live and in the studio. Another thing that made me happy about it was that you could imitate, to a certain extent standard instruments and, apart from that you could create new and fresh sounds. I had already been trying to get different sounds out of the Hammond organ, I had exhausted all those possibilities. Not only do I view music from a harmonic sense, I view it as a noise source as well and at that particular point it was all welded into one thing. There was an instrument which could do all of that and more; it had endless possibilities. As I said, there were lots of problems taking it around on tour. The first oscillators were a little weird. The problem in tuning is not so great now. The instrument I have is not designed to take on the road. It was originally designed for studio use. It's been toughened up and it's been customised and dealt with; huge power supplies and things have all been changed to cope with whatever problems we've come up with."

Clearly ELP weren't reluctant to experiment. Palmer was quoted in *Hit Parader* in January 1972; "I've tried an electronic drum kit and for what it's worth it's just not worth bothering with. I'm not too mad on freaking out my drums on stage — I prefer a natural drum sound."

After *Pictures At An Exhibition*, Emerson remained a strong advocate for the possibilities he had yet to explore with the Moog. He was quoted in *The New York Times* in December 1973; "I suppose my act did become really physical (with The Nice) and I was discovering weird ways to use and expand the range of the Hammond. Emerson, Lake and Palmer has cooled down somewhat on this side now. It may have been necessary to become showmen then but now I think we can afford to exaggerate the music a bit more. I use two Hammonds, one for playing and the other for, if you like, stunting. Most of the early physical business was discovered by accident. I'd knock over an instrument and in the crashing, some weird sound would come out which we worked into the act. Just over five years ago, I made the breakthrough when I learned of this instrument with the bigger range — I was using the two organs then, standing up between them. It was the Moog synthesiser and I've been adding keyboards since then. I don't think it is possible yet to get most of the keyboard sounds that I want, that I sense, out of just one keyboard, like crossing a Steinway with a Hammond. Rock technology is just not yet advanced enough. Maybe some day, but in the meantime I have my thirteen keyboards and Carl is working on a set of synthesised drums."

Emerson was quoted in *Beetle* in February 1974; "I've had so many hassles with orchestras and working with musicians' unions, and trying to get the whole thing together. I haven't yet come across an orchestra which is that helpful. If I can do it all myself, then I'll do it, I'll get the instruments to make the biggest sound I can, and do it that way. There's a conductor who's a great friend of mine and who's into doing something like this with me in the future. He has the capabilities of getting an orchestra together that I would like to work with. I shall wait until that happens. An orchestra itself should be used as an orchestra, there's a lot in one hundred people all playing together, it's a lovely sound. It's just all the hassles that come with it. I've done it on lots of occasions. Each time there have been problems with the union. You don't get time to rehearse it or anything. It costs an awful lot. For a start, the musician has to finance it himself. We could handle it now, but at the time that I did it with The Nice, I couldn't afford it. I had to go to the Arts Council to ask them to finance it. It's a joke when you see them turning up. They don't bother to ask for their music. They sit there with the newspaper on their stand, they really do. They're like kids, they muck about. The conductor we had was really trying to get them working. They just wouldn't co-operate."

As a fan, it's easy for me to say "*Pictures At An Exhibition* was brilliant, if you did that without an orchestra then surely it's proven that one isn't a necessity to do justice to another round of ideas?!" but fairly enough, it's likely the case that ELP didn't see things this way at times.

Lake was quoted in *Circus* in August 1977; "We won't be tempted by people who say, 'Oh man, why don't you clean up? Just make another five or six albums of the same junk and then

A Continuing Legacy

retire to the south of France?' Well, we don't want to retire. I want to be a singer the rest of my life. It would be a waste of my talents and what I have to say, and also a waste of this band's position — because, you know, we're very lucky people to be able to afford to do something like this with the orchestra and all this expense. We're probably one of the only bands in the world in that position. I met Dave Brubeck's son recently, Chris Brubeck, and he said to me, 'Thank God you've done it, man' and we said, 'Done what?' And he answered, 'Putting the orchestra together, it's just fantastic.' The orchestra is fantastically powerful — more than a Moog synthesiser could ever be. It will shake buildings. We weren't satisfied with the power of electronic instruments. They were not dynamic enough. They didn't give us the vehicle to play the music we wanted to write, and that's why we find ourselves here today, in this precarious position. Obviously, we realise the risk in taking this orchestra on the road. It could be financially disastrous. We've invested everything we've ever made into this project and nobody's given us any guarantees. We're alone out there and only time will tell if it was all worth it."

It is understandable as to why ELP were often accused of being overly ambitious. Emerson was quoted in *Gig* in September 1977; "I'd have definitely gone with an orchestra on my own if the group hadn't. I didn't want to go back on the road unless there was an orchestra. I needed a change, a challenge. It was either strip everything down to the basics, like, no thirteen keyboards, just possibly bass, piano and drums. Go that route, or one step further than what we'd ever done before. I chose the one step further. Everybody laughed when I mentioned it. They said, 'you're crazy, it'll never pay.' They've been proved right. But it's working."

Lake was quoted in *Gig* in September 1977; "The emphasis now is on the music. I'm aware of the appeal of what we've done in the past in terms of theatrics, but it doesn't dominate us as a group and I don't think it dominates our presence in the audience's mind. In the past we've been so involved with electronic music. Why shouldn't I work with an orchestra? Do you have to be a certain age? Frank Sinatra works with an orchestra and nobody

ELP - *Pictures At An Exhibition*: In-depth

questions it. The future of ELP would have been very limited if it had been only an electronic future. We've exploited that to its fullest extent. The future had to become broader, there had to be something more to achieve. The stunt now is the music."

To which the journalist considered; "And the 'stunt' works, with or without the orchestra. *Pictures At An Exhibition* sounds better than ever, given greater dramatic shading by the orchestra, while 'Nut Rocker' still proves just how well ELP can genuinely rock and roll. In fact, they rocked so hard in New York that Emerson got carried away with the excitement and played the piece again. The audience did not complain."

Palmer was quoted in the same feature; "We didn't want to come zipping back with the same old show. An orchestra seemed like a natural progression. It all works, but ELP would work without the orchestra. The orchestra is just the cream on top of the cake. Actually just the cherry in the middle. It's time for people to invest in the music. What goes on the record is most important. You can't see smoke bombs and revolving drum kits on the record."

Still though, the later half of the seventies was shaky ground for ELP in some ways. Palmer was quoted in *Gig* in September 1977; "Our record sales haven't been as big as they should be. We figured when we came back we'd be bigger than when we left. In actual fact the double album price is expensive, ticket prices are high and our overheads are astronomical. We've got everything against us. After seven years of being together we really don't want to end up broke. I'd like to be a pioneer as much as my pocket will let me."

Financially, they probably weren't joking! It was reported in the same feature; "Experimentation has never been cheap. Although there's probably more artistic credibility in spending money on an orchestra than on an inflatable flying pig, it's still expensive. The show with orchestra was costing at least $2 million to keep on the road. ELP definitely aren't laughing all the way to the bank."

Palmer was quoted; "I'm actually broke. This is purely an artistic thing. After six years on the road we figured it was time to rethink our musical policy. We had to leave England for artistic reasons, which is unusual. Most groups leave England for financial gain."

To which Emerson was quoted; "I've never been one to check on how much it would cost or how long it would last. Obviously I had a feeling that we couldn't afford to last out the tour with the orchestra. But it came as a bit of a shock when our manager walked in the dressing room one night before the show and said we had to stop the orchestra. We had to go out as a three piece, there was no other choice. We had our manager with a shotgun behind us saying, 'Look, if you don't play as a three piece, forget it, you'll be bankrupt'."

It is fascinating to think that ELP had, at least to an extent, not been happy with what they could achieve musically as just a three piece. But then again, any artist needs to do what feels right to them at any given time. Lake was quoted in the same feature; "I know what I like. Any artist knows their taste. We play rock 'n' roll really well. But we were at a stage in our career where just to play rock 'n' roll would have been very enjoyable but not serious enough. We enjoy rock 'n' roll. We could quite easily make a rock 'n' roll album at any time and enjoy it and get artistic rewards from it. Real ones. But when we stopped touring three years ago that wasn't a possible alternative. We could now."

Lake was quoted in *Circus* in August 1977; "This band runs on the cooperation between us. That element is the power of ELP. It's the combination and the battles between that romance of mine and that technical development of Keith's which makes this an interesting and exciting group. Not that it wouldn't be just as valid and exciting if Keith were to do a strictly instrumental thing or if I were to do a complete album of simple songs, but at this moment this is the way it is and right now we're committed to that, because being in a band isn't something you enjoy. It's not a fairground ride. It's something you're a part of creatively and it's often a very painful experience, if you're sincere. The reality of being in a band like ELP is an artistic reality, it's not an entertainment reality. For promotional purposes it would be great to say, 'Yeah, we had a fantastic time making this album' — but we didn't."

An endearing aspect of ELP is that each individual had their own distinct musical interests. In such regard, what they achieved as a group when it came to *Pictures At An Exhibition* is noteworthy. Emerson was quoted in *Beetle* in February 1974; "I've been trying to get a solo album for ages and ages. For about a year I've got about five tracks done, in bits and pieces which I like, and I think that will continue. Whenever I like something, I want it for ELP, because that is my prime objective. It's not really that important to me because I am doing what I want to do. Usually, solo albums are done because the cat is not being allowed to do what he really wants to do. All of us do whatever he wants on stage, and on record, so there is no real hurry."

With regards to the scope of ELP doing solo albums, Lake was quoted in *New Musical Express* in November 1973; "They'd just be made up of things we felt we couldn't do within the band. Maybe Keith would get into some specialist piano things — twenties boogies or something. Things like that would be better on more personal albums. I don't know whether we'll do it. It'd just be as a kind of hobby if we did."

Lake was quoted in *Circus* in August 1977; "If I wasn't in ELP, if I was on my own, I wouldn't sound like this at all. It would be all singer-oriented music. It would be all simple songs. But that's part of what ELP is all about. We're a blend of all types of elements. On my own I wouldn't necessarily change the classical bent. I'd still be interested in using orchestration because it's an incredible emotional medium to work with, but I'd concentrate on singing because that's where my future lies. In a musical sense, I think that's the only talent I have. I mean, I play guitar, I play bass, and it works out okay, but it's nothing great, nothing I want to dedicate my life to. It's hard as a singer working with a band like ELP because so much of the music is written by Keith and his songs are instrumentally-oriented, which makes it very difficult to find the vocal line. But again, there's a good and a bad side to it. Strictly from a singer's point of view, it's harder work, but it also gives you a special experience you wouldn't have otherwise.

A Continuing Legacy

That's why it's valid for me at this point to do it. When I sing in 'Pirates' or 'Karn Evil 9', the phrasing is complex, whereas in something like 'Lucky Man', it's completely natural. But, you see, in any group situation you have to have compromise and co-operation, which defuses the natural source of the energy. You get a less pure but more colourful product in the end. I'm in a strange position in this band because I see things from two sides, and that can make working in the group a very frustrating experience. I see it from a composer's side and from a singer's side, while Keith really only sees it from a composer's side. My work in some circumstances, then, has to be more imposed and for Keith it's completely natural. Keith and I write quite differently. For me, songwriting is a very direct path between an immediate thought and the final product. There's very little self-conscious thought in between. You virtually end up with what you started with, and the strength of the song is based almost completely on that initial inspiration. The music of ELP is less dependent on that initial inspiration and more dependent on the subsequent work and development of that thought."

And who's to say that having the ambition and scope to do solo projects is a bad thing anyway? Emerson was quoted in *Circus* in March 1972; "This band is designed so that everybody gets featured equally. I think it's working out that way; we're all getting recognised in our own right and we're very pleased about that. That's why we're called Emerson, Lake and Palmer. The fact is, if we want to do our own projects, then we have a chance."

Overall, the musical rapport between everyone in ELP was undeniable. Palmer was quoted in *Disc* in October 1972; "I think I'd probably be Greg's mate even if I didn't play with him, you know what I mean? It's that kind of deal."

To which Lake was quoted; "We've always got on, on that sort of level. Arguing just never occurs because we both see things almost exactly the same way and you never have to argue with somebody like that. (Keith is) more a loner than I am or Carl is but the three of us spend an awful lot of time together."

Palmer was quoted; "Keith is the kind of cat who, if we're

ELP - *Pictures At An Exhibition*: In-depth

all at a party grooving away he comes along and it's not a bad vibe. He'll get in in his own sort of way. He's sort of slow getting into the social trip. He's always got things to do. He gets himself totally together, like he'll disappear for hours and do things."

Whilst there was an extent of pressure on ELP that resulted in a reluctance to release *Pictures At An Exhibition* as an album, it continued to be the case that such pressures perhaps didn't subside even in later years of the band's tenure. Palmer was quoted in *Hit Parader* in January 1972; "At first we were lumbered with that superstar trip and we had to fight very hard to overcome it. I know that from the beginning we were given a very good break but I can tell you we really had to prove ourselves. Thankfully it seems as if we've been accepted but it doesn't stop there. Once you've been accepted you can't slow down. That's the time you've really got to work harder simply because there's so much more to fight for. Nowadays you've really got to stay on the ball, especially with all these new guys coming along."

It was stated in *New Musical Express* in November 1973; "ELP have always been one of those bands to provoke sharp differences in opinion. They win polls with immaculate ease. Commercially they're one of the world's biggest. Yet they're still often presented in print as a sort of soulless juggernaut, a lumbering musical monster."

Lake was quoted in the same feature; "You can make it without an image. It's been true with us and I suppose it's unusual. I mean, some rock success is sustained by image alone. All the David Bowies and T. Rexes involve a tremendous amount of image control, based a lot on how they appear to people. As for how we appear to the people, I've no idea at all — not a clue. But although we don't have an image as far as the press are concerned, we're very much a people's band. In the beginning we got hit hard by the press and we've tended to shy away ever since — maybe that's why we're faceless in a way."

The success of *Pictures At An Exhibition* inspired a revival of not only classical music itself, but of other interesting interpretations of it. In May 1972, the *Reading Evening Post* advocated of the

A Continuing Legacy

B. Bumble and the Stingers single 'Nut Rocker'; "Ah yes, sweet memories. This was in the charts ten years ago... This has probably been revived because of the success of Emerson, Lake and Palmer's version in their live concerts. A timeless bopper."

In the *Pictures At An Exhibition* 2016 liner notes, Chris Welch quoted Lake; "Sales of orchestral versions of *Pictures At An Exhibition* increased for the next couples of years. People must have gone out after hearing the ELP album wanting to hear the original. A lot of today's classical musicians say they were inspired to play after hearing our album and that's quite an honour."

Such was the impact of ELP's *Pictures At An Exhibition*, it could be considered that it inspired a revival of Mussorgsky's piece. When performed by other musicians, ELP's version was often used as a point of comparison. Tomita's version of *Pictures At An Exhibition* was compared to ELP's in the *Coventry Evening Telegraph* in September 1975; "Mussorgsky's work has appeared in many forms — from the original piano work though to orchestral music by Ravel to the rock version by Emerson, Lake and Palmer. But Tomita has added a new dimension to this dramatic work, taking us on a magical mystery tour of the world of Moog. And yet the framework and spirit of the original are strictly adhered to, so that while Tomita exploits the possibilities of the synthesiser to a far greater extent than did Keith Emerson, this new version remains a more disciplined and less indulgent work. Tomita may lack the emotional fire required of a true virtuoso, but he is doing a splendid job of mapping the vast musical territories created by the Moog."

The review advocates that in Tomita's version, the Moog is certainly the dominant instrument and more so than in ELP's version. However, that's not to say that Emerson's use of the Moog in ELP's version was any more or less expansive; to use the Moog as part of an ensemble is not necessarily to negate or neglect the full scope of what the instrument is capable of. Really, both ELP's and Tomita's versions of *Pictures At An Exhibition* are worthwhile pieces of musical innovation and exploration. They both have their merit as an interesting take on Mussorgsky's original piece. This is the case in terms of working with the possibilities of the

ELP - *Pictures At An Exhibition*: In-depth

Moog and in the general sense of doing something creative with an already iconic piece of classical music.

Lake enthused; "The success of our adaptation helped tear down the walls of prejudice and bigotry that had until then helped maintain the belief that you had to be either extremely clever or upper class, or preferably both, in order to be able to enjoy classical music. It was perhaps the first time that a young rock audience had ever been offered up an honest, serious attempt at performing a piece of classical music with a rock sentiment and a rock feeling, but not in a corny piss-taking way. It was a real attempt to make it sound good and relevant, and they appreciated it. Following the reaction and enthusiasm shown that night by the young audience from Newcastle, and the surprising success of the record, it was clear that, at least to some small extent, the world of classical music would never be quite the same again. The sale of formal orchestral versions of *Pictures* rose significantly after our record was a hit, and they were being bought by people who had never listened to classical music before. Now of course, classical music is used from everything from mobile phone ringtones to the warm-up music for sporting events in stadiums to TV adverts. We all pretty much now take it for granted, but it wasn't like that in the early seventies when we released *Pictures At An Exhibition*. Despite the fact that we never actually foresaw that kind of musical liberation taking place, and that it was an accident rather than intentional — we were just playing music we wanted to play — our contribution to that has now become quite a rewarding legacy for us. Personally, I'm not really convinced that I have any great talent or that I have ever had any specific plan — I just want to entertain — but we were there in the right place and at the right time. I'm just a lucky man."

In deciding to do their own version of *Pictures At An Exhibition*, ELP made a strongly informed choice. Not every iconic piece of music was deemed suitable to be given the ELP treatment. Emerson was quoted in *Keyboard* in November 2010; "Once, we tried to record Booker T.'s 'Green Onions'. I don't know whose idea it was, but there's only one 'Green Onions', and

A Continuing Legacy

that's Booker's version. Even the great Jeff Beck said it's one of the most difficult tunes even though it's such a seemingly simple riff. You hear every bar band play 'Green Onions' and you're like, 'Oh, get out!' But if anyone shouldn't go there, it's ELP!"

For an album that nearly wasn't released and was often subject to uncertainty from the band themselves, ELP's *Pictures At An Exhibition* certainly made its mark. Emerson; "As the album didn't cost much to make, Greg said 'Let's put it out for £1' so I rode up to my nearest shop in the Kings Road, Chelsea, on my Norton 750 and bought my own album for a pound. I parked my motorbike, went in to buy a newspaper and the LP, came out and I got a parking ticket from a traffic warden! But the album got nominated for a Grammy Award and it's amazing to think that so many musicians got into classical music from hearing ELP's *Pictures At An Exhibition*. It broadened their whole musical horizon."

In recent years, Carl Palmer has played some of the ELP classics with his new band. He was quoted in *Prog* in May 2017; "The legacy (of ELP) is important, and I've looked after it in what I think is the most honest way, I'm out there playing the music. In my band, I didn't want to replace Greg or Keith and I didn't even want a keyboard player, but we can reproduce the sound quite closely. It shows you a different flavour and the versatility of ELP's music. It's the way to go for me and I'm enjoying it. I like the musical depth I have with my own band. It's really uplifting to play some of the ELP stuff, like *Pictures* and *Tarkus*. It's all rewarding and I do feel that someone has to keep it going, so here I am."

Lake was quoted in *Beat Instrumental* in January 1971; "I want someone in two hundred years' time to pick up an ELP album and say 'Christ, that's a gas!'" Well, at the time of writing this book, ELP's *Pictures At An Exhibition* album is nearing its fiftieth anniversary so here's to the next one hundred and fifty years.

Pictures At An Exhibition – A Comprehensive Discography

Album Personnel

Emerson, Lake & Palmer
Keith Emerson — pipe organ, Hammond (C3) and L100) organs, Moog modular synthesiser (ribbon controller), Clavinet
Greg Lake — bass guitar, acoustic guitar, vocals
Carl Palmer — drums, percussion

Credits
Producer: Greg Lake
Engineer: Eddie Offord (credited as Eddy Offord)
Remastering: Joseph M. Palmaccio
Arrangers: Keith Emerson, Greg Lake
Recorded using the Pye Mobile Recording Unit
Cover design: William Neal
Cover painting: William Neal
Artwork: William Neal
Photography: Nigel Marlow, Keith Morris
Lyrics: Greg Lake, Richard Fraser

Track Listing

Side One
1. 'Promenade' (Modest Mussorgsky, arranged by Keith Emerson) 1:58
2. 'The Gnome' (Mussorgsky, Carl Palmer) 4:18
3. 'Promenade' (Mussorgsky, arranged by Greg Lake) 1:23
4. 'The Sage' (Lake) 4:42
5. 'The Old Castle' (Mussorgsky, Emerson) 2:33
6. 'Blues Variation' (Emerson, Lake, Palmer) 4:22

Side Two
7. 'Promenade' (Mussorgsky, arranged by Emerson) 1:29
8. 'The Hut of Baba Yaga' (Mussorgsky, arranged by Emerson) 1:12
9. 'The Curse of Baba Yaga' (Emerson, Lake, Palmer) 4:10
10. 'The Hut of Baba Yaga' (Mussorgsky, arranged by Emerson) 1:06
11. 'The Great Gates of Kiev' (Mussorgsky, Lake) 6:37
12. 'Nut Rocker' (Tchaikovsky, Kim Fowley, arranged by Emerson, Lake, Palmer) 4:26

2001 Remaster Bonus Track
13. 'Pictures At An Exhibition' (Studio version)*
'Promenade'
'The Gnome'
'Promenade'
'The Sage'
'The Hut of Baba Yaga'
'The Great Gates of Kiev'

* The studio version, recorded in 1993, was released on *The Return Of The Manticore* box set and some pressings of the 1994 album *In The Hot Seat*.

2016 Deluxe Edition

Disc One - Original 1971 album - 2016 remaster - plus bonus
1. 'Promenade' (Modest Mussorgsky, arranged by Keith Emerson) 1:58
2. 'The Gnome' (Mussorgsky, Carl Palmer) 4:18
3. 'Promenade' (Mussorgsky, arranged by Greg Lake) 1:23
4. 'The Sage' (Lake) 4:42
5. 'The Old Castle' (Mussorgsky, Emerson) 2:33
6. 'Blues Variation' (Emerson, Lake, Palmer) 4:22
7. 'Promenade' (Mussorgsky, arranged by Emerson) 1:29
8. 'The Hut of Baba Yaga' (Mussorgsky, arranged by Emerson) 1:12
9. 'The Curse of Baba Yaga' (Emerson, Lake, Palmer) 4:10
10. 'The Hut of Baba Yaga' (Mussorgsky, arranged by Emerson) 1:06
11. 'The Great Gates of Kiev' (Mussorgsky, Lake) 6:37
12. 'Nut Rocker' (Tchaikovsky, Kim Fowley, arranged by Emerson, Lake, Palmer) 4:26
13. 'Pictures At An Exhibition' (Medley) 'Promenade' (Instrumental)
'The Hut of Baba Yaga'
'The Curse of Baba Yaga'
'The Hut of Baba Yaga'
'The Great Gates of Kiev' (Bonus track - Live at the Mar Y Sol Festival Puerto Rico 4 December 1972)

Disc Two - Live at the Lyceum Theatre on 8 December 1970
1. 'Promenade' (Mussorgsky) 2:02
2. 'The Gnome' (Mussorgsky, Palmer) 5:41
3. 'Promenade' (Mussorgsky, Lake) 1:24
4. 'The Sage' (Lake) 5:07
5. 'The Old Castle' (Mussorgsky, Emerson) 4:24
6. 'Blues Variation' (Emerson, Lake, Palmer) 6:05
7. 'Promenade' (Mussorgsky) 1:31
8. 'The Hut of Baba Yaga' (Mussorgsky) 1:15
9. 'The Curse of Baba Yaga' (Emerson, Lake, Palmer) 4:56
10. 'The Hut of Baba Yaga' (Mussorgsky) 1:11
11. 'The Great Gates of Kiev/The End' (Mussorgsky, Lake) 6:52
12. 'The Barbarian' Béla Bartók, (arranged by Emerson, Lake, Palmer) 5:23
13. 'Knife-Edge' (Emerson, Lake, Leoš Janáček, Johann Sebastian Bach, Richard Fraser) 8:03
14. 'Rondo' (Dave Brubeck, Emerson, Lee Jackson, David O'List, Brian Davison) 17:50
15. 'Nut Rocker' (Tchaikovsky, Fowley) 4:26

Country By Country

This includes all known variants from the UK, USA, Germany and Japan.

UK
Original 12th November releases:
Island, HELP1, LP
Island, ZCI 9177, cassette
Island, Y8I 9177, 8 track cartridge

Reissues:
Manticore K 33501, LP, 1973
Manticore K433501, cassette, 1973
Manticore K833501, 8 track cartridge, 1973
Essential / Castle Communications ESM CD 342, GAS 0000342ESM ACO, CD, 1996
D2 Vision DVDP001, DVD, 1999
Twin sided CD/DVD disc with audio CD on top side and film of original live concert from 1970 on a DVD on the flip side.
Castle Music CMRCD167, CD, 2001
With bonus track of studio version.
Classic Pictures Entertainment DVDP002, DVD, 2003
Collectors Edition
Sanctuary Midline SMRCD057, CD, 2004
With bonus track of studio version.
Sanctuary Records 1776980, 2CD, 2008
Deluxe edition including bonus track.
BMG / Manticore   BMGCAT2CD3, 2CD, 29th July 2016
Deluxe edition.
BMG BMGCATLP3, LP, 29th July 2016

USA
Original 4th January 1972 releases:
Cotillion ELP 66666, LP
Cotillion M56666, cassette
Cotillion M 86666, 8 track cartridge
Cotillion Records M 6666, open reel

Reissues:
Cotillion TP 66666, 8 track cartridge
Atlantic SD 19122, LP, August 1977
Atlantic CS 19122, cassette, August 1977
Cotillion 19122-2, CD, 1986
Victory 383 480 018-2, CD, 1993
Rhino Records R2 72225, CD, 1999
Shout! Factory 826663-10492, CD, 26 June 2007
Razor & Tie 7 93018 34001 4, LP, 2013
Record Store Day picture disc, limited edition of 1250.
BMG BMGCATLP3, LP, 29th July 2016

Germany
Original releases:
Island Records 85 804 ET, LP, 1971

Reissues:
Manticore 87 226 ET, LP, 1973
Manticore 54739 YT, cassette, 1973
Manticore 46 406 5, LP, 1983
Manticore 68 660 0, cassette, 1983
Cotillion 19122-2, CD, January 1984
Manticore 87 226 ET, LP, 1984
Atlantic 7567-81521-2, CD, 1987
Classic Pictures Entertainment DVDP002, DVD, 1999
D2 Vision DVDP002, DVD, 2001
Twin sided CD/DVD disc with audio CD on top side and film of original live concert from 1970 on a DVD on the flip side.
Cotillion Speakers Corner Records, ELP 66666, LP, 2004
Sanctuary Records 1776980, 2CD, 2008
Deluxe edition including bonus track.
BMG / Manticore   BMGCAT2CD3, 2CD, 29th July 2016
Deluxe edition.

Japan
Original release:
Atlantic   P-8200A, LP, 1972
Atlantic   YSA1040A, cassette, 1972

Reissues:
The LP was reissued in 1974 and 1976 with the same catalogue number as the original release but with different obi strips.

Atlantic   P-6363A, LP, 1980
Cotillion, Atlantic 19122-2, CD, 1984
Cotillion, Atlantic 32XD-372, CD, 28th November 1985
Atlantic 20P2-2049, CD, 10th September 1988
Warner-Pioneer Corporation 6P1-2049, LP, 1988
Victory VICP-23104, CD, 21st November 1993
Manticore, Victor VICP-60635, CD, 3rd March 1999
Victor VICP-62116, CD, 21st November 2002
Victor VICP-41203, CD, 22nd September 2004
Victor VICP-63173, CD, 28th September 2005
Victor VICP-64236, CD, 25th June 2008
Victor VICP-64564, CD, 24th September 2008
Victor VICP-64642-3, CD, 28th January 2009
With bonus Lyceum recording.
Victor VICP-70150, CD 23rd June 2010
Victor VICP-75059, CD 23rd May 2012
Victor VICP-78003, CD, 23rd April 2014
With bonus track of Rondo.

SINGLE
Despite the nature of the album, a single was released in USA and Japan. It was also released in Canada, Australia, New Zealand, Argentina, Brazil and Mexico.

Nut Rocker / The Great Gates Of Kiev
Cotillion 44151, 1972, USA
Nut Rocker / The Great Gates Of Kiev
Atlantic P-1128A, 1972, Japan

Tour Dates

What follows are all of ELP's know tour dates from the outset, leading up to the recording of *Pictures At An Exhibition* and continuing through to the end of 1971, its year of release. Courtesy of Mark Scalise at ELPArchive.com

1970
Sunday 23rd August — Guildhall, Plymouth, England
Saturday 29th August — Afton Down, Isle of Wight Music Festival, England
Friday 4th September — Open Air Love & Peace Festival, Germany
(ELP were originally scheduled, but did not perform)
Saturday 19th September — Winter Gardens, Malvern, England
Monday 21st September — Civic Hall, Wolverhampton, England
Thursday 24th September — Town Hall, Watford, England
Friday 25th September — City Hall, Hull, England
Saturday 26th September — Starlight Rooms, Boston, England
Sunday 27th September — De Montfort Hall, Leicester, England
Monday 28th September — Guildhall, Portsmouth, England
Thursday 1st October — Town Hall, Leeds, England
Sunday 4th October — City Hall, Newcastle, England
Wednesday 7th October — The Dome, Brighton, England
Friday 9th October — Greens Playhouse, Glasgow, Scotland
Sunday 11th October — Caird Hall, Dundee, Scotland
Friday 16th October — Northeast London Polytechnic, London, England
Saturday 17th October — Brunel University, Uxbridge, England
Monday 19th October — Colston Hall, Bristol, England
Tuesday 20th October — Winter Gardens, Bournemouth, England
Wednesday 21st October — Town Hall, Birmingham, England
Sunday 25th October — Fairfield Hall, Croydon, England
Monday 26th October — Royal Festival Hall, London, England
Tuesday 27th October — City Hall, Sheffield, England
Wednesday 28th October — St. George's Main Hall, Liverpool, England (cancelled)
Sunday 22nd November — St. George's Main Hall, Liverpool, England
Saturday 28th November — Kongresshalle, Frankfurt, Germany
Sunday 29th November — Circus Krone, Munich, Germany
Monday 30th November — Nuremberg, Germany
Tuesday 1st December — Konzerthaus, Vienna, Austria
Wednesday 2nd December — Sporthalle, Böblingen, Germany
Friday 4th December — Limmathaus, Zurich, Switzerland
Monday 7th December — Free Trade Hall, Manchester, England
Tuesday 8th December — St. George's Hall, Bradford, England
Wednesday 9th December — Lyceum Strand, London, England
(*Pictures At An Exhibition* filmed)
Saturday 12th December — Leeds University, Leeds, England
Sunday 13th December — Kinetic Circus, Birmingham, England

1971
Thursday 4th February — Guildhall, Southampton, England
Thursday 4th March — ABC, Stockton, England

Friday 5th March	ABC, Hull, England
Saturday 6th March	ABC, Lincoln, England
Sunday 7th March	The Regal, Cambridge, England
Wednesday 10th March	Capitol, Cardiff, Wales
Friday 12th March	ABC, Plymouth, England
Sunday 14th March	Civic Hall, Wolverhampton, England
Wednesday 17th March	Odeon, Cheltenham, England
Thursday 18th March	Big Apple, Brighton, England
Sunday 21st March	ABC, Blackpool, England
Monday 22nd March	Free Trade Hall, Manchester, England
Tuesday 23rd March	St. George's Hall, Bradford, England
Wednesday 24th March	City Hall, Sheffield, England
Friday 26th March	City Hall, Newcastle, England
	(*Pictures At An Exhibition* album recording)
Sunday 28th March	Odeon, Lewisham, England
Monday 29th March	Winter Gardens, Margate, England
Tuesday 30th March	Guildhall, Portsmouth, England
Thursday 1st April	ABC, Wigan, England
Friday 2nd April	Green's Playhouse, Glasgow, Scotland
Saturday 3rd April	Caird Hall, Dundee, Scotland
Tuesday 6th April	Winter Gardens, Bournemouth, England
Wednesday 7th April	De Monfort Hall, Leicester, England
Thursday 8th April	St. George's Hall, Liverpool, England
Friday 9th April	Odeon, Birmingham, England
Wednesday 21st April	Theil College, Greenville, PA, USA
Friday 23rd April	Eastown Theatre, Detroit, MI, USA
Saturday 24th April	Eastown Theatre, Detroit, MI, USA
Sunday 25th April	The Spectrum, Philadelphia, PA, USA
Tuesday 27th April	Stanley Theatre, Pittsburgh, PA, USA
Wednesday 28th April	Fairleigh Dickinson University, Teaneck, NJ, USA
Friday 30th April	Fillmore East, New York, NY, USA
Saturday 1st May	Fillmore East, New York, NY, USA
Sunday 2nd May	Painters Mill Music Theatre, Owing Mills, MD, USA
Monday 3rd May	Shea Theatre, Buffalo, NY, USA
Thursday 6th May	Loews State Theatre, Providence, RI, USA
Friday 7th May	Viking Memorial Hall, Upsala College East Orange, NY, USA
Tuesday 11th May	Guthrie Theatre, Minneapolis, MN, USA
Wednesday 12th May	Milwaukee Arena, Milwaukee, WI, USA
Friday 14th May	Public Hall, Cleveland, OH. USA
Saturday 15th May	Community War Memorial, Rochester, NY, USA
Sunday 16th May	Alexandria Roller Rink, Alexandria, VA, USA
Wednesday 19th May	Kiel Opera House, St. Louis, MO, USA
Friday 21st May	Wabash College Gymnasium, Crawfordsville, IN, USA
Saturday 22nd May	Cincinnati Gardens, Cincinnati, OH, USA
Sunday 23rd May	Memorial Gym, Kent State University, Kent, OH, USA
Monday 24th May	Ohio Theatre, Columbus, OH, USA
Wednesday 26th May	Carnegie Hall, New York, NY, USA
Thursday 27th May	Hatch Memorial Shell, Boston, MA, USA
Friday 28th May	Convention Center, Wildwood, NJ, USA
Sunday 30th May	Bucknell University, Lewisburg, PA, USA
Wednesday 2nd June	Schwarzwaldhalle, Karlsrhue, Germany (rescheduled to 6/17)

Saturday 5th June	Sporthaus, Zoffingen, Switzerland
Sunday 6th June	Zurich, Switzerland
Monday 7th June	Konzerthaus, Vienna, Austria
Wednesday 9th June	Circus Krone, Munich, Germany
Thursday 10th June	Stadthalle, Offenbach, Germany
Friday 11th June	Meistersingerhalle, Nuremberg, Germany
Saturday 12th June	Concertgebouw, Amsterdam, Netherlands
Sunday 13th June	Phillipshalle, Dusseldorf, Germany
Monday 14th June	Weser-Ems Halle, Oldenburg, Germany
Tuesday 15th June	Stadhalle, Offenbach, Germany
Wednesday 16th June	Musikhalle, Hamburg, Germany
Thursday 17th June	Schwarzwaldhalle, Karlsrhue, Germany
Sunday 20th June	Royal Theatre Drury Lane, London, England
Saturday 17th July	Sports Arena, San Diego, CA, USA
Sunday 18th July	Berkeley Community Theatre, Berkeley, CA, USA
Monday 19th July	Hollywood Bowl, Los Angeles, CA, USA
Friday 23rd July	Agrodome, Vancouver, BC, Canada
Saturday 24th July	Paramount Theatre, Portland, OR, USA
Friday 30th July	Music Hall, Houston, TX, USA
Saturday 31st July	Municipal Auditorium, San Antonio, TX, USA
Wednesday 4th August	Municipal Auditorium, Atlanta, GA, USA
Friday 6th August	Pirates World, Dania, FL, USA
Saturday 7th August	Pirates World, Dania, FL, USA
Monday 9th August	Charlotte Coliseum, Charlotte, NC, USA
Tuesday 10th August	The Dome, Virginia Beach, VA, USA
Thursday 12th August	Stanley Park, Toronto, ON, Canada
Friday 13th August	Place De Nations, Montreal, QC, Canada
Saturday 14th August	Convention Hall, Asbury Park, NJ, USA
Sunday 15th August	Convention Hall, Wildwood, NJ, USA
Wednesday 18th August	Onondaga County War Memorial, Syracuse, NY, USA
Thursday 19th August	Peace Bridge Center, Buffalo, NY, USA
Friday 20th August	Hara Arena, Dayton, OH, USA
Saturday 21st August	Auditorium Theatre, Chicago, IL, USA
Sunday 22nd August	Syria Mosque, Pittsburgh, PA, USA
Tuesday 24th August	Wonderland Gardens, London, ON, Canada
Wednesday 25th August	National Arts Centre, Ottawa, ON, Canada
Thursday 26th August	Boston Common, Boston, MA, USA
Saturday 28th August	Public Auditorium Cleveland, OH, USA
Monday 30th August	Bushnell Memorial Hall, Hartford, CT, USA
Tuesday 31st August	Alexandria Roller Rink, Alexandria, VA, USA
Wednesday 1st September	Gaelic Park, New York, NY, USA
Saturday 13th November	The Spectrum, Philadelphia, PA, USA
Sunday 14th November	Auditorium Theatre, Chicago, IL, USA
Monday 15th November	Eastown Theatre, Detroit, MI, USA
Tuesday 16th November	Eastown Theatre, Detroit, MI, USA
Wednesday 17th November	Eastown Theatre, Detroit, MI, USA
Friday 19th November	Hirsch Memorial Coliseum, Shreveport, LA, USA
Saturday 20th November	The Warehouse, New Orleans, LA, USA
Monday 22nd November	Municipal Auditorium, Atlanta, GA, USA
Thursday 25th November	Madison Square Garden, New York, NY, USA
Friday 26th November	Civic Arena, Pittsburgh, PA, USA

Saturday 27th November	Farm Show Arena, Harrisburg, PA, USA
Sunday 28th November	Richmond Arena, Richmond, VA, USA
Monday 29th November	Lyric Theatre, Baltimore, MD, USA
Tuesday 30th November	Music Hall, Boston, MA, USA
Wednesday 8th December	City Hall, Newcastle, England
Thursday 9th December	City Hall, Sheffield, England
Friday 10th December	Free Trade Hall, Manchester, England
Saturday 11th December	Capitol, Cardiff, Wales
Monday 13th December	Pavilion, London, England
Tuesday 14th December	Pavilion, London, England (early show)
Tuesday 14th December	Pavilion, London, England (late show)
Wednesday 15th December	Pavilion, London, England
Friday 17th December	Caird Hall, Dundee, Scotland
Saturday 18th December	Empire, Edinburgh, Scotland
Sunday 19th December	Green's Playhouse, Glasgow, Scotland (early show)
Sunday 19th December	Green's Playhouse, Glasgow, Scotland (late show)

In-depth Series

The In-depth series was launched in March 2021 with four titles. Each book takes an in-depth look at an album; the history behind it; the story about its creation; the songs, as well as detailed discographies listing release variations around the world. The series will tackle albums that are considered to be classics amongst the fan bases, as well as some albums deemed to be "difficult" or controversial; shining new light on them, following reappraisal by the authors.

Titles to date:

Jethro Tull - Thick As A Brick	*978-1-912782-57-4*
Tears For Fears - The Hurting	*978-1-912782-58-1*
Kate Bush - The Kick Inside	*978-1-912782-59-8*
Deep Purple - Stormbringer	*978-1-912782-60-4*
Emerson Lake & Palmer - Pictures At An Exhibition	978-1-912782-67-3
Korn - Follow The Leader	978-1-912782-68-0
Elvis Costello - This Year's Model	978-1-912782-69-7
Kate Bush - The Dreaming	978-1-912782-70-3

Forthcoming:

Jethro Tull - Minstrel In The Gallery	978-1-912782-81-9
Deep Purple - Fireball	978-1-912782-82-6
Deep Purple - Slaves And Masters	978-1-912782-83-3
Talking Heads - Remain In Light	
Jethro Tull - Heavy Horses	
Rainbow - Straight Between The Eyes	
The Stranglers - La Folie	
Alice Cooper - Love It To Death	